# Simply Amuck

Also by the author:

*Amuck: Tales From a Hobby Farm*
*Beyond Amuck: More Hobby Farm Adventures*
*Haiku for the Soul*

# Simply Amuck

## Life on a Hobby Farm

## Sue Stein

CALUMET
EDITIONS

Minneapolis, Minnesota

**CALUMET EDITIONS**

Minneapolis, Minnesota

FIRST EDITION

SIMPLY AMUCK
Copyright © 2024 by Sue Stein.
All rights reserved.

This is a work of fiction. All of the characters, names, incidents, organizations and dialogue are either the products of the author's imagination or are used fictitiously.

Printed in the United States of America.
10 9 8 7 6 5 4 3 2 1

ISBN 978-1-959770-04-6

Book design by Sue Stein

Cover image: iStockPhoto/Shootingstar22
Goat clipart: Pixabay.com
Image page 117 © Annette Herman
All other images © Sue Stein

*For Anita*
*All the letters we wrote to each other when we were kids—*
*You're the reason I'm a writer*

# Contents

## Chapter 1

# It's Not Paranoia if They Really Are Out to Get You...

It was nearly dark outside at four-thirty in the afternoon—that's November in Minnesota for you. Adding to that state of affairs was the delightful twenty-five-degree "high" temperature, and it was no wonder I was loaded for bear. My dog, Breezy, a smooth-coated collie/God-knows-what-mix had barreled into the living room in a frenzy of loud barking, launched herself onto the couch, and looked out the window, her head swiveling like Linda Blair in *The Exorcist.*

"*What now?*" I muttered as I got my lazy butt off the kitchen chair and went to look outside. I had been attempting to have a phone conversation. *Good luck with that.* I scanned the yard, didn't see anything, and once I had hung up the phone, turned to the still-barking Breezy, "I don't see anything. What are you barking at now? Good lord!"

She managed to look chastened and lay down on the couch. I went back to my chair, sat down, and decided to do some work on the computer. Soon enough, I heard it. Dogs have far better hearing than humans, so it did take me a while to catch on to what Breezy had been barking about. Yes, the damn coyotes were in full-throated yipping and howling mode. Now I was *really* mad. After all these years living here, I truly detest coyotes. I used to think they were kind of cute—in a bloodthirsty, feral way. I flung open the door to the porch and was regaled by the noise. Stepping outside onto the back patio in the delightful frigid evening, I could tell they were close—at least two of them, calling to each other, back and forth. Enough was enough.

"SHUT UP!" I roared. And they actually listened. They may have been deafened, now that I think about it because I really let 'er rip. I stood out in the freezing cold and glared out to the pasture. I didn't know exactly where they were hunkered down, but I had total certainty I was being watched. I called them a few very bad names to see what they'd do—nothing. Since I have totally and completely *had it* with all members of the coyote family, I decided it was time to call their bluff. "You and me? Guess what, suckers. You are in my cross-hairs." I raised my right hand and made my thumb and forefinger into the shape of a gun. "BOOM!" I said as I pretended to blast them to smithereens, my hand jerking up in the air like the recoil from a .44 Magnum. The movie *Dirty Harry* comes to mind. I wish I had also snarled, "So, you have to ask yourself...*do I feel lucky?* Huh, punk?" in my best Clint Eastwood imitation.

After blowing away the coyotes with my awesome imaginary firepower, I glared out into the growing dark, daring them to mess with me. Not a peep came from the pasture, pole barn, or woods. I turned on my heel and stalked to the door. Turning back to look at where I assumed they were hiding, I had to get one more dig in. "You want some hand-to-paw? *Bring it.*" After lobbing that last bit of verbal napalm, I went back inside the house, hoping none of the neighbors across my back forty had heard me. Really—can you imagine what I was like *before* I went through menopause and was in full-on PMS-mode? I'm much nicer now.

Perhaps you might think I was a tad overdramatic—these were only *coyotes* I was talking to, after all. Or maybe that I went a *little* bit off the deep end. No, I would have to completely disagree with you there. After countless run-ins with coyotes and untold years of stress from worrying about them attacking my dogs, chickens, mini horses, and goat, not to mention *me*, I've earned every bit of anger and, yes, I'll say it—downright loathing I feel toward their kind. And I'm a huge animal lover.

The next morning, I was wide awake and figured there was no point in rolling over for the umpteenth time to try to get back to sleep. I removed myself from my toasty warm blankets and went to make coffee. Looking at the clock on the stove, I realized it was only 3:45 in the morning. Ugh. That's just wrong.

I peeked out the curtains to see an inch or two of snow had fallen during the night. The thing I really like about winter is that the snow-covered ground helps so much to light up the night. Even on the darkest and most moonless nights, if some type of foul creature

All manner of tracks crossing my front pond heading to my house.

is traversing the yard, I'll be able to spot its movement against the white background and take appropriate countermeasures. When spring finally comes, I admit to a sinking feeling when the last bits of snow melt because that means the critters are once again invisible as they make their nightly rounds. It helps immeasurably to know what's coming to get you…and, most importantly, that *it is coming to get you.*

## Chapter 2

# Hammock Heaven

Lazing the day away in the hammock is a long-standing tradition at my house. The inaugural first "hammock" began in 2005, a gift to myself after I finally graduated from college—it had only taken me twenty-seven years. In my defense, my original major was Geology. Everything was going wonderfully until I came up against an implacable foe: Calculus. Derivatives? Integrals? Theorems? After my head exploded one too many times, I switched my major to English and then settled in for a leisurely part-time journey on my way to two bachelor's degrees. Plus, I absolutely loved school. Yeah—*I'm one of them.* My dog Shay, long since departed, loved to hop up on the hammock with me and snoozed as I read a book while I also periodically snoozed along with her. She was the sweetest dog but could turn into a stone-cold killer when defending her territory. A lot like me, actually. I miss her.

Flash back to the present: I was looking forward to a long-awaited interlude in the hammock on a sunny afternoon. First, I made sure

I had all the necessary items for a successful hammock experience: blanket, pillow, book, and my dog Breezy. "Come on, Breezy! Let's hammock!" She raced over, and we happily hopped up on the hammock and settled in for a relaxing day. The chickens were out in their run, having fun chasing bugs, while six tom turkeys were wandering around out in the horse pasture. I read in peace for a while until the turkeys raised a ruckus. It's always something around this place. I put my book down and looked out to the pasture and saw two deer leaping and figured that was what had upset the turkeys. Rather than taking a leisurely nap like usual, Breezy had been suspiciously alert, watching the edges of the woods, her head turning as she scanned. I figured she was monitoring the turkeys. I should have known something else was going on.

Soon enough, she leaped off the hammock with her fiercest bark and ran to the pasture. I couldn't see what she was after because I was doing 360's in the hammock. I was tossed to the ground, my butt hitting hard. While aloft and spinning before impact, I screamed at her, "God! No! Stop! *What the hell?!*" and then *Splat!* I hit the ground.

On my hands and knees in the dirt, I watched Breezy. Her hackles were raised as she growled and barked. The weeds in the pasture were too high for me to see what was out there, but it had to be a coyote. I lurched to my feet and staggered in her general direction. "Damn you, coyote!" followed by, "Breezy, get back!"

The stinking thing had ruined an idyllic hammock interlude. Breezy came, sat, and stayed as I went barefoot into the chicken yard (yuck!) to lock them securely in the coop. As I walked back to the house, I hurled insults over my shoulder at the lurking coyote. "Damn thing! Don't be thinking you chased us out of the yard. Hell no, we were *planning* on going into the house!"

I peeked back to be sure it wasn't stalking me while still maintaining my hard-ass attitude. "You can *sooooo* bite my ass, coyote.

I'm not afraid of you." I suddenly realized what I had said. I had given it a bald-faced invitation *to bite my ass*. I had meant it as a throw-away line, but to any self-respecting, slavering coyote, it could be interpreted as a come on. *Sure lady, I'd be happy to take a chomp off of your ample behind.* Breezy and I hurried inside before it made its move.

After nearly daily coyote sightings, Breezy and I had severely neglected the hammock. Finally, on a cool August afternoon, I decided: *Time to hammock!* and Breezy and I settled in for a nap.

Alas, it was not to be. I was awakened repeatedly by a red squirrel loudly chewing something on the nearby roof, probably a black walnut. I couldn't see it anywhere so I turned over in the hammock and tried to ignore it. It leaped from the hole it had made in the eaves and scampered onto the branch of the black walnut tree next to the house. I should trim that damn tree. It nestled on a branch above us and commenced loudly complaining about something. Maybe its interior remodeling of my attic wasn't going well. Who knows? Breezy glanced up periodically, ready to pounce. Eventually it lay down along the limb and its sleepy eyes closed. I tried to nap, but the squirrel had ruined that for me; instead, I read for a while—a really good thriller. That got me all keyed up, and I couldn't hang out there any longer. I decided to get up and do something productive.

I went to tackle the mass of dead branches I'd tossed into a pile at least two years before, and had to drive the lawnmower around every time I mowed, which tended to annoy me to no end. Toss, pull, yank, move branches to another pile to someday burn it all. Maybe in another two years. I need to work up to stuff like that.

Breezy was now under the hammock in the hole she'd dug. Suddenly, she gave one loud bark and glared at the woods at the very back of the yard. It had to be another infernal coyote. Unfortunately, I was a sitting duck if I stayed where I was—I'd be cut off from the house and have to make for the pasture if it came for me. I supposed I could sprint up to the pole barn and make my last stand there. *Screw that!*

Since there had been so many coyote sightings lately, I went to retrieve my trusty baseball bat that I'd left next to the hammock just in case. I grabbed the bat, told Breezy to stay and she actually did. I stalked across the side yard, scanning the woods. Coyotes are really good at camouflaging themselves, and I couldn't see it. I put Breezy in the house and decided to go all Rambo and strut around on my patio with bat in hand since the back door to the house was readily accessible if it streaked toward me with its gaping maw ready to chomp on me. "Come and get me, sucker!" I taunted it. After a while, with no response from the coyote, I decided to pack it in and went to grab the blankets from the hammock. My hands full, I dropped the bat. Bad idea. I was a bit nervous as I reached down to retrieve it while watching for movement in the woods.

Even in my fear, I realized I absolutely would go down fighting if I were attacked. I wouldn't screech in terror and run away. I'd scream in challenge and run toward it. And pray. And swear.

Every so often I come across online articles like these:

"Woman Strangles Rabid Fox Attacking Her in Backyard." The article opens by saying, "A woman trying to fend off a rabid fox that was biting her in the leg reached down with one hand to hold shut its mouth and with the other strangled it. 'I couldn't do anything else to get it away from me. I don't like to kill anything.'"

"Georgia Woman Strangles, Kills Rabid Bobcat After It Attacks Her." The article continues, "'It caught me slightly on my face, but I got him before he could do much damage. I took it straight to the ground and started inching my hands up to its throat. I knew that was the only way I was getting out of this,' she recalled."

Whenever I read these articles, I first think, *That is awesome! She is so like me. I would totally do that.* And then I think, *Wow, no wonder I'm still single.*

## Chapter 3

# Mouse in the House

Felix, my new kitten, had been living with us for about a month. He was nearly twelve weeks old and still tiny. Late one night after lights out, he was playing under a table in my bedroom and it was keeping me awake. I finally kicked him out, shut the door, and blissfully slept until morning when I heard his tiny "mew mew" outside the bedroom door. I took pity and got up to let him in and then climbed back under the warm covers. He rappelled

Felix at 12 weeks old.

up the side of the bed using his claws on the blankets, climbed on top of me and kissed me. Then, he went right back under the table as he had done several hours earlier and soon commenced making just as much noise.

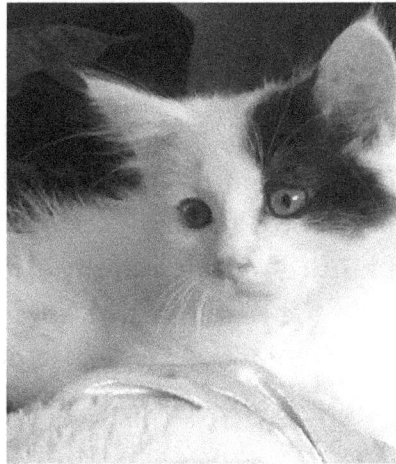

"That's what got you in trouble before," I muttered. He kept at it, and, realizing that I would not get back to sleep again, I got up in the early morning gloom, barely able to see. I stumbled over to the table and, squinting down to the floor, saw what looked like one of his little toys underneath. I could barely make out a long tail and almost reached out to grab it out of his paws, but something stopped me. Some very wise part of me managed to snatch my hand back before I touched it. I made it over to the wall and switched on the light and returned to the table. Ugh. It was a thoroughly chewed and quite dead mouse. I suppose I should have congratulated him since it was his very first mouse—and at such a tender age! And then I remembered he had kissed me with that mouth after dispatching the rodent. *Gaahhhhh!*

Several nights later, I was awakened in the middle of the night by Felix jumping up on the end of the bed. It was too dark to see what he was up to, but I knew it was no good. Suddenly, I realized what he was doing—he was playing with another mouse. *On my bed.* I had no idea if it was alive or dead, but that made no difference. Instinct took over, and both of my feet kicked upward from under the covers and I launched him and the mouse off the end of the bed. He jumped right back up, and I launched him again. I hurried to throw off my blankets, got up, slammed the bedroom door tight, and turned the lock in case he had figured out how to open doors. He's pretty smart, and I wouldn't put it past him. I turned on the light, knelt down on the floor, and peered under the bed to make sure he wasn't lurking underneath with his new friend. Somehow, I levered myself back upright and stumbled back to the warm covers where the other cat, Nutter, was purring and we went back to sleep.

The prior winter had brought the usual influx of mice into my house. They must come in through the garage along the heating pipes and up into the rest of the house. I saw them boldly running around the floor while my cats slept nearby. The mice must have known they were safe. The cats I had at the time were lazy and didn't want to lift a paw. They never did a thing about the mice until the day I said, "What the hell? *You are cats.* You are supposed to catch mice! Catch them, dammit!" Soon enough, hunting began in earnest. See, they understand me.

The next morning, I got up to find one of the cats had thrown up in the hallway. It looked like it was some kind of a worm or something else gross in it, so I put it all in a baggie, took it to the vet, and asked them what the hell it was. Believe it or not, it was mouse guts and also a little foot and some mouse fur in with it. When they told me that, I just about barfed.

That night, as I walked down the hallway, I noticed something new on the floor. Bending down to look more closely, I realized it was a baby mouse's tail and part of its leg. Two down, and God knows how many more to go. At least the cats got off their furry little butts and started exterminating the invading vermin.

That was all fairly well disgusting, but Nutter had more excitement in store for me. I'm not sure if he thought it was funny or not—you never know with him. I could tell he'd caught a mouse and was playing with it somewhere in the house. Either that or it was one of his toys. I'd given up at that point on the whole mouse situation and decided it was safer to continue sitting in my recliner with my book and a cup of tea, or maybe it was a big glass of wine. That sounds more like it. Eventually, the knocking and dragging noises ended and I settled in with my book. A few hours later, I decided it was time for bed. I can read for eight hours straight—or longer. I've always been like that, even as a kid. When the last Harry Potter book came out, UPS delivered it at nine in the morning, and my dog, Shay, and I went right to the hammock and stayed there the entire day and part of the evening, getting up only occasionally for food, water, and the bathroom. I read the whole damn book that day, and it was a huge book, but it was so good. I look back at that day as one of my favorites. Shay did, too.

On the night Nutter caused the excitement, I got ready for bed and snuggled in under the covers. Nutter curled up in my arms, purring, and we fell asleep. Sometime in the middle of the night, he had gone off somewhere, maybe to kill another mouse. I rolled over and pulled the covers closer. *What was that soft little thing I just touched?* I wondered groggily. I tried to fall back asleep, but it started bugging me. Did one of the cats put a toy in my bed? When I reached out in the dark and touched it again, I leaped upward with a scream. I threw off the covers and lurched over to the light switch. I went back to the bed and pulled the blanket back to reveal *a dead mouse.* Nutter had left it for me. What a guy. Can you imagine waking up with that next to you in bed? I know some of my old boyfriends weren't exactly winners, but good lord—even they would be better to wake up next to than a dead mouse. Thinking back…maybe not. I would actually take the mouse over several of them.

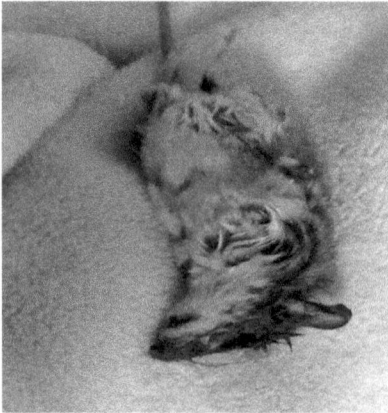

How would you like to wake up next to this?

Before I could go back to bed, I stripped off all the blankets and threw them in the wash, grabbed new bedding, and remade the bed. Do you think I could sleep after that? Nope. I went out to the living room and watched TV until the sun came up. That night and for many nights after, I checked under the covers before I would get into bed. Nutter watched me, probably snickering to himself.

# Chapter 4

# I Wanna Be a Momma

The second oldest chicken, Violet, had been sitting on one lonely little egg for weeks. I knew it wasn't hers—she was twelve years old. Most chickens have an expiration date of about eight years. Violet was *ancient* and hadn't laid an egg in years. Hens stop laying eggs after only a few years and very few chickens make it to Violet's advanced age. She has good genes: her mom, Celeste, was still going strong at thirteen.

Normally, it takes twenty-one days for an egg to hatch, with the hen sitting on it each day and only leaving briefly for food, water, and bathroom breaks. I knew the egg wasn't fertile and would never hatch—Reggie was the only rooster left, and he was too old. No way he could have performed. And I didn't want poor Violet to have to make such a herculean effort for nothing.

Violet might have been old, but she was bound and determined to be a first-time mom. Each time I went to the coop, there she was in the nest box on her egg, focused on hatching that egg and having a baby chick to call her own.

I remembered seeing a sign at the feed store that they were going to have chicks for sale the next day. On one of my trips to the coop, I went over to Violet in her nest box and asked her if she really wanted a baby. She perked up on her egg, looking at me with hope. I told her I'd try to find her one.

The next day, I went to the feed store to pick out a little chick. Violet is a Silkie chicken, so I chose a little grey ball of fluff, also a Silkie. I was hoping it would turn out to be a hen and not a rooster, but I wouldn't know for several months. If it crowed after a few months, then I'd know for sure. The tiny chick was placed in a little cardboard box for its trip to its new home. Once at home, I had to hurry up and get the baby situated because it was the season finale of *Supernatural* on TV, and no way was I going to miss watching Dean Winchester. Yum!

I dug around in the garage and found the bottom of a small plastic dog kennel. Digging some more, I found a brooder lamp to keep the chick warm. I spared a moment to go up to the coop to let Violet know that she would meet her baby in the morning. All the chickens were snuggled in for the night, but Violet, sitting on her egg, listened.

Back in the house, I got the baby all set up in the bottom half of the kennel, with a soft dog toy to snuggle up to, a towel beneath, with moistened chick food and water for its first meal. I placed a window screen on top of the kennel and the brooder heat lamp above that, then I tucked the little chick in for the night and turned off the room's light and sat down in front of the TV with minutes to spare before *Supernatural* started.

It didn't take long: the chick was all alone in the dark for the first time in its brief life and wanted everybody to know about it. Who knew something that tiny could be so piercingly loud? I could barely hear the TV over its incessant cheeping. I couldn't blame it for being scared. I turned the volume up to full blast to drown out the piteous sounds. After a while, it slept.

The new chick is to the right,
snuggling on a furry dog toy.

Next morning, I let it run around on the dining room floor. My cat, Nutter, sniffed it—my cats and dogs amazingly enough, have never tried to eat any of the chicks over the years, although Kerwin, another cat, did sniff longingly, eyes closed, mouth slightly agape, directly over the head of one chick. He was thinking about it, that's for certain.

The baby followed Nutter around the room, maybe thinking he was its mom. I put the chick back in its kennel and went back to the garage to retrieve the extra-large kennel where there'd be plenty of room when the chick was united with its new mom, Violet. I walked out to the coop. Violet was in the nest box, on her lonely little egg. "Time to meet your baby!" I told the other chickens she'd be back in a few days with her new baby as I scooped her up and went out the door.

Once in the house, I set Violet on the floor and went to get the baby out of its kennel and let it run around. The baby saw Violet right away and darted over to her, peeping mightily the entire way. Violet eyed her and began "purring." I thought she liked the chick, but I stayed close in case she decided otherwise. Nutter and Breezy came into the room to observe the touching moment. "Violet, here's your baby," I said, "You're a mom now!"

The baby and Violet got to know each other there on the floor. I looked over to Breezy and I swear it looked like she wanted to be a mom, too. She had a wistful expression on her face. Pushover that I am, I said, "Okay, maybe we can get a puppy one of these days, and you'll be a mom, too." Satisfied, she left the room and hopped up on the couch for a much-needed nap.

I picked up Violet and put her in the kennel. I caught the baby as it skidded around on the linoleum, looking for Violet, and placed it in the kennel, also. Settling down on the floor next to the kennel, I watched as they bonded. It was so cute. The chick toddled up to Violet, who nuzzled it with her beak. She showed it how to eat and drink, clucking the whole time. Everything was going well. The baby snuggled her way under Violet's wing to sleep, Violet tucking her gently underneath with her head. I went to sit in a chair and nearly cried. It was so darn heart-warming. *She's twelve years old,*

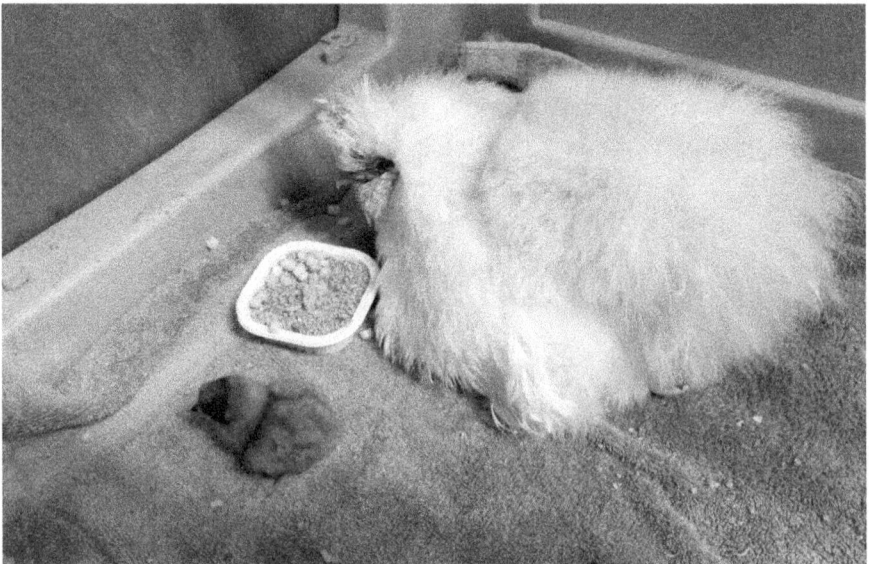

Violet and her baby soon after they met.

*ancient in chicken years, and now she's a first time mom,* I thought. I'm such a sap. But if you were there, you would probably have shed tears of happiness for Violet and her baby, too.

Eventually, mom and baby were ready to go back to the rough-and-tumble of the chicken coop. I carried them up there inside a small kennel and set it on the coop floor. The other chickens gathered around and peered in while the baby chick hid under Violet. I let them all get used to each other before I opened the kennel door. Violet's mom, Celeste, had missed her while she was gone and was at the front of the milling mass welcoming her back. The two had always been inseparable, and Celeste seemed to be happy to see her.

Violet and her newborn stepped out of the kennel and I warned the other chickens to leave them alone. Over the years, I'd observed how protective and fierce hens could be with their chicks and how interesting it was that some of the roosters also actively interceded to keep the chicks safe. Other roosters were only interested in chasing hens around for a little fun. Just like human men, I concluded.

Violet had always been an assertive hen, and I had no worries about the other chickens bothering her or the chick. All my chickens have nicknames, as do my cats and dogs. At times I'd called her Violina and, when she was being more aggressive than assertive, she was dubbed Violent. She can be a bruiser when she chooses.

Over the next few days on my coop visits, I noticed that Celeste was becoming more and more despondent. Violet was having nothing to do with her. Celeste would toddle up to Violet and want to be friends, and Violet would turn her back on her. I felt horrible for Celeste. This was all my fault—I'd thought I'd been making Violet happy by making her dream come true, but I'd also created a nightmare for her mom, Celeste.

One morning, Celeste again tried to get Violet's attention, making piteous noises. I turned to Violet and said, "What the hell is the matter with you, Violet? She's your mom. She raised you.

She's been there for you for all these years and now that you have a baby of your own, you turn your back on her. That's terrible. Be friends with her, that's all she wants. She missed you and now that you're back, you ignore her. That sucks."

I picked up Celeste and hugged her to my chest, petting her. "I'm sorry, Celeste. I had no idea she was going to be such a bitch to you. I feel awful about it. But I still love you." I gave her one last hug and set her down. Violet turned her back on her and walked away, baby chick in tow.

The next morning, I went out to the coop to feed the chickens, only to discover Celeste dead in the corner. I have no doubt that she died of a broken heart. I looked over at Violet, tears brimming in my eyes. "Look, Violet—*look right over there!* Your mom is dead. *She is dead.* All you had to do was pay a little bit of attention to her, but no, you refused. You finally had your baby, and you decided you didn't need her anymore. I hope you're happy. She loved you and you did that to her. Let's hope your baby doesn't do the same thing to you when it grows up." I bent down and picked up Celeste's body and told her how sorry I was, even if she couldn't hear me. I took her from the coop to bury her.

Fast forward to a year later. The chick turned out to be a hen, and I named her Sable for her black feathers. The few other hens and Reggie, the rooster, had succumbed to old age, and only Violet and Sable were left in the big coop. And now Sable was brooding on a clutch of unfertilized eggs, wanting to be a mom at a year old. You'd think I'd learn from past mistakes. No, are you kidding? I don't. I keep making the damn things. Of course, I asked her, "Sable, do you want to be a mom? What about you, Violet? You could have another baby." It looked to me like they were interested, but that could simply be me putting ideas in their heads, like usual.

This time, I ordered chicks from a hatchery in Texas. I would normally have purchased them from the feed store in town, but the pandemic had forced the closure of most businesses. On a warm day in April, the chicks arrived. This hatchery didn't have a minimum order of chicks—most required you to purchase twenty-five chicks at a time. That was way too many. This place, for whatever reason, said that you could mix and match chicken breeds as long as it was thirty-three dollars or more. Scanning their website, I chose a mixture of five Silkies, two black and white speckled Japanese bantams, and two white Frizzles, which have curly feathers. I love bantam chickens. I've had the regular size chickens and much prefer the little ones. Kind of like my miniature horses—I like the little ones better than the big horses.

I briefly considered putting them all in the extra-large dog kennel together and letting them get a bit bigger before introducing them to their soon-to-be new moms, but that was going to be too much work for me to keep clean with nine chicks. Instead, I brought the cardboard box containing the chicks to where Violet and Sable were waiting. The chicks were making a fearsome noise, cheeping all together.

I set the box down, and before I opened it to let them all out, I turned to Violet. "How many chicks do you want? One? Or do you think you can handle two? You are kind of old, maybe one would be best." I looked at Sable. "Looks like you get to raise the rest. Do you think you're up for that?" They both looked at me in alarm. Maybe I hadn't told them previously how many chicks were soon to arrive. *My bad.*

I opened the box to let the little buggers out, and they swarmed madly around like a hive of angry bees, with high-decibel peeping. Several arrowed straight over to Sable while the rest targeted Violet.

Suddenly, both chickens had panicked looks on their faces. Violet ran and hid in the corner. Sable pecked at the chicks milling around her. Both of them looked up at me as if to say, *What in God's name were you thinking? This is too much!*

I kept an eye on the proceedings to make sure no chicks were harmed while I busied myself with setting out small chick waterers and feeders. I had to remove the regular water dish because the chicks could fall in and drown. That had happened once in the past and I actually did learn from that particular mistake. There's hope for me yet. I squatted down and discussed the situation with the two chickens. "Okay, Violet. It looks like you really don't want to be a mom anymore. That means you, Sable, are going to have to pick up the slack. You have nine chicks to raise. Time to step up and be a mom." I left the coop to let them sort it all out.

An hour later, I went back to see how things were going. Sable had all nine of them snuggled underneath her. I don't know how they all fit, but they did. She was cooing in contentment. Violet, meanwhile, was keeping her distance, muttering darkly.

As the days progressed and the chicks grew larger, Violet and Sable got into a few dustups. I wasn't sure what was going on. Was Violet jealous that Sable had all the babies? Who knows what goes

Sable with, believe it or not, nine chicks under her,
along with wood shavings on her head.

on in chickens' brains? I can't figure out what goes on in my own. Eventually, I had to separate them with a wire panel. The square openings in the panel were large enough for the chicks to dart through, but Sable and Violet were separated. I decided they would figure things out sooner or later.

The chicks began spending more time with Violet than with Sable, who paced along the other side of the panel, muttering to herself. Soon, they were sleeping underneath Violet instead of Sable. The mutiny was complete. The lines had been drawn, and sides had been chosen. Violet was now the mom of all nine of them, and Sable was alone. God knows what that was all about, but that's what happened. I removed the wire panel, and no fights broke out. Sable refused to interact with the babies any longer and began laying eggs again. That sealed the deal—hens don't lay eggs or brood on them if they already have chicks. Grandma Violet was now raising her daughter Sable's kids, as sometimes occurs with people.

The more I know about animals, the more I see people doing the same exact things; I find it ironic and also humorous. People think they are superior to animals, yet they do the same damn things in the same damn ways. Yet they never realize it because they don't bother to look closely at animals, nor do they really care. After all, as the majority of people would think—we're *humans*, not lowly *animals*. Yeah, right.

The nine chickens turned out to have only two roosters and seven hens—statistically the ratio should have been 50/50. I lucked out there, and the roosters get along together fine. As time went on and the chicks grew up into teenagers, turf wars broke out. At first, Violet and Sable ran the roost and claimed the best food dish. They chased the kids away whenever they dared approach the food. After a few months of this, I went out to the coop to see Violet and Sable hiding behind the small kennel I'd left out there. Sometimes, chickens like to get away from everybody else, and the kennel serves that purpose. The kids had staged a coup, and Violet and Sable were now lowest on the pecking order. I placed new food dishes behind the kennel and commiserated with them. Violet is now nearly fourteen, and she really doesn't need to put up with crap from snot-nosed kids, but, once again, because of my misguided intentions, there have been unforeseen consequences. Will I never learn?

## Chapter 5

# Something Got Your Goat?

On an early evening stroll with my dog, Breezy, and Donald, the goat, both on leashes, we walked to the end of the road. In the distance, coming our way, I saw two people, a small dog, and what looked like two mini-Doberman pinschers. The previous night on our walk, Breezy had been too wild when she saw her dog friend, Sydney, who lives at the very beginning of our road. Sydney had been walking with her owners toward us and Breezy yanked me all over the place when she realized who it was.

Not wanting to go through a replay of that, especially with a stubborn goat along, when I saw the people, dog, and whatever-else-it-was approaching, I decided it would be a good idea to turn around and start back home.

I attempted to wrangle the dog to my left and the goat to my right to follow me. That's when I heard one of the people shout, "Sue! Sue! Come meet my baby goats." It was my neighbor, Dan, and his girlfriend, walking their small white dog and two adorable baby Nubian goats with velvety, floppy ears. Donald is an Alpine mix and has upright ears. The baby goats walked docilely behind Dan, trailing their leashes.

Donald, now a strapping two-and-a-half-year-old, towered over them. Tiny "*Baa baas*" emanated from the babies. Donald ignored the baby goats. He was more interested in the little dog—he was fascinated by it. I guess Donald thinks he's a dog. Wondering whether the goats had been gelded, I asked Dan, "Have the babies been…" and I made a "snipping" motion with my fingers.

He knew right away what I meant. "Oh yeah, they put a rubber band around them [the testicles] and pretty soon they drop right off."

"Ugh! That has got to hurt," I said, cringing.

"No, it's okay," Dan replied.

I gave a meaningful glance to his girlfriend and looked back at him as I said, "Oh, *really?*"

She looked amused and turned to him, "Yeah, like we should try it on you and see if it hurts." Dan wisely chose to completely ignore us while we cackled.

Dan loves Donald, who returned the favor by licking his nose and nuzzling him. Everyone loves Donald. It must kill Breezy not to be the center of attention.

While we stood there, several cars drove past and the people goggled to see three people, two dogs, and three goats having a neighborly chat on the gravel road. Dan has lived on our road nearly as long as my family. My parents built the house I now live in back in 1963. Dan's family built in the early 1970s. A few of us long-timers are still left, sprinkled with a few new people, but the basic country-like character of our neighborhood is exactly like it was when I was a kid, growing up in the '60s, which' is exactly how we all like it.

Goats are fascinating, intelligent creatures. They can be maddening as well and, with their intense curiosity about the world around them, they tend to get into everything.

Donald was running loose in the yard again while Breezy and I wandered around looking at weeds to pull, grass to cut, wood piles to burn. I could go on and on about all the things that need to be done around here, but simply talking about it is exhausting. Thinking about actually doing any of it? No way. That would drive me straight to the hammock to recover from the trauma.

As the dog and I meandered around the yard, I noticed that Donald was eating my flowers on the front patio. I had gotten wise to his voracious appetite, and before letting him run free, I had put my favorite flowerpots inside the house out of his sight. I had tried to stop him from gobbling all the flowers, but he's too stubborn. Duh! *He's a goat.* I went inside, held up the succulent hibiscus plant and cackled with glee as he pawed furiously at the glass storm door, lusting for a taste. "*Nyah, nyah. You can't have this one!*" I taunted. "*Bwahahahahaha!*" He stopped pawing for a second and looked up at me. In a huff, he turned and scampered down the steps and

Poor Donald—I dress him up for the holidays.
Here he has reindeer antlers and an elf collar.

raced out into the yard, letting me know that I wasn't victorious—
he could get into plenty of other things out there.

Like the day the mailman drove his mail truck down the driveway to my house to deliver a package. I was monitoring Donald as
he ran pell-mell around the front yard when the truck pulled up next
to me. The mailman hopped out with the package and introduced
himself, and we started chatting. Turned out he was friends with
Dan, my neighbor, so he was already familiar with being around
goats. Meanwhile, Donald had jumped up into the mail truck and
commenced munching on first-class mail. Plenty of junk mail was
there for the taking, but no, he glommed onto the good stuff.
Typical. I tried to pull the mail out of his mouth while wrestling
him out of the truck. "Donald! No! Stop! That's a felony!" He kept
on munching. The mailman laughed and said, "I wouldn't care so
much if it was third-class mail" as I finally dragged Donald bodily
out of the truck. I can only imagine what the recipient of that
particular letter thought when they noticed goat-mouth-sized
chomp marks on the envelope.

Having any type of animal, including livestock, means vet visits
and the attendant bills. Over the years, I've racked up impressive
amounts for dogs, cats, mini horses, and alpacas. Donald the goat
was the sole outlier, but that was soon to change.

Not long after meeting Dan's goats, Donald was acting odd. He
wasn't being his normal pissant self. I researched online to see if
I could figure out what might be wrong, but there was too much
information. Time to call in the big guns. I checked with Kim, the
owner of the local feed store. She gave me her sister-in-law's phone
number, who also had goats. I phoned her, and she gave me the
number of her goat vet. There don't seem to be many vets who will
work on goats in my area, maybe because not many people *have*
goats. I always was the one who had to be different. This veterinary

clinic was located way down in Zumbrota—a nice little road trip of about fifty miles one way. *Who cares?* I thought. *This is Donald!*

I made an appointment for a day later and then started thinking about how I was going to get him down there. I now owned an SUV, which would make things easier. Previously, I had a four-door sedan and yes, I ferried an alpaca back and forth to the University of Minnesota Large Animal Hospital in St. Paul. In the back seat. That story is in my first book, *Amuck*.

Since Donald wasn't yet full-grown, he would be able to squeeze into an extra-large dog kennel. I grabbed it out of the garage and got it ready to go, placing straw in the bottom. Then I called my niece to see if she would be able to help in the morning to lift the kennel into the back of my SUV once I had wrestled him inside it.

The next morning, I led Donald out of his garage and over to the kennel. I wanted to get an early start because I didn't know how long it would take to shove his ornery little butt into the kennel. It was easier than I thought. All I needed to do was toss in a huge chunk of Romaine lettuce, and *voila!* he ran right in there to gobble it up, and I slammed the door shut. Once my niece showed up, we each lifted one side and heaved him up into the car, and off Donald and I drove on our road trip.

At first, he was nervous and complained, but once he realized he was in this for the duration, he was a champ for the whole car ride. He looked out the window the whole time, enjoying the view.

It was a nice drive, and eventually, we pulled into the veterinary clinic. I'd never seen one like this before—

Donald in his kennel.

livestock barns and corrals everywhere with cattle trailers and semis parked here and there. It was a weird place but kind of fun. The small building to the far right seemed to be the main office. I parked in front and went inside.

The vets came outside, and we lifted Donald's kennel out of my car and set it on the ground. I had his collar and leash ready and slipped it around his neck as he emerged from the kennel, looking around at everything. We all went inside the office, and his exam was done right there in front of the desk. I hadn't realized this was a large-scale livestock auction type of operation with a veterinary clinic on site, but it made sense since it was deep in farm country, nearly to Rochester, Minnesota.

As she looked Donald over and checked his vitals, the vet turned to me and said, "This is the healthiest goat I've ever seen." I guess they were used to huge farms with tons of goats with all the attendant health problems. Donald decided right about then that the office floor was a great place to drop some goat pellets. I apologized, but she said, "No, it's great he did that, now we can check his stool for worms," and she scooped up a few pellets and went to examine them.

Donald and Felix get to know each other.

He did have a few minor problems and she prescribed anti-inflammatories. He had lice, which she said was normal for goats. The office call was $10, which included the exam. The anti-inflammatories were $6.50. His CBD vaccination was fifty cents. If they didn't have a $48 minimum charge, the whole thing would have only cost $23.20.

As I wrote out the check in shock, I thought they were kidding when they told me the total cost. I've never gotten out of a vet visit anywhere for less than $150. It was worth the fifty-mile one-way trip. If I had to take him to the University of Minnesota Large Animal Hospital like I had with Lombardo, an alpaca, it would have cost several hundred dollars or more just for an exam. I cringe when I remember how much I spent on him there.

Oh, and she trimmed all his overgrown toenails—for free. We loaded Donald back into the kennel and lifted him into my car and off we went. It was a fun road trip and I think Donald enjoyed getting out and seeing new things and meeting new people. He's a total people person—for a goat.

## Chapter 6

# Hang on Tight

Several years ago, I was better at taking the dog for a daily walk, even in the depths of winter. Breezy and I would walk to the end of the road and turn back. It may have been during January that I first noticed something odd high up in a tree a ways off the road. Each day as we walked past, I would squint up at it and try to figure out what the heck it could be. Was there an odd growth on that limb that I had never noticed? Could an animal possibly be perched in the same exact spot each time we passed by? What the heck *was* that thing?

After about a week, the sun must have finally been in the optimal position because I figured out what I was looking at. A raccoon. Specifically, a very *dead* raccoon. I stopped in my tracks and stared up at it. A huge raccoon had somehow died in the oddest position—he was lying on his stomach on the large branch, his arms and legs hanging on each side of the limb, rather a precarious perch. It looked like he was sleeping. It was the weirdest thing. I shook my head and we continued our walk.

Just hanging out...

The next day, he was still there. And the day after that. Weeks went by, and the raccoon hadn't moved. Well, duh. He was *dead*—of course he wasn't going to *move*. It came to be sort of a game for me: would the raccoon still be hanging there in the tree? Or would today be the day he had plummeted to the ground and been lost in a snow bank? I looked forward to my glimpse of the poor, dead, stiff thing. Yeah, I know—rather macabre, but I found it amusing in a dark sort of way.

February passed, and then March. Still the raccoon valiantly hung on. I was surprised that nothing had tried to eat it. You'd think the crows or owls would have had a field day on that sucker. He was huge. And I wondered—why did he die? Why did he die *there?* Was he rabid? Did he crawl forty feet up that huge tree, clamber out onto the limb, lay down to sleep, and never wake up? I started to feel sorry for him. *Poor raccoon!* What a way to go.

The snow melted, the trees began to bud, and still he hung on. As April's cold showers turned to May's rampant flowers, the weather became hot and humid. Walking past that section of the road became rather fragrant as the raccoon began to heat up. I held my nose and hurried past, while Breezy wanted to linger and sniff the enticing smell of months-dead raccoon.

I wondered when he gave up his death grip, would he plummet to earth in one piece or several?

I never found out because one day, he had simply disappeared. Forty feet below his precarious perch lay a babbling brook filled with long grasses. I imagined him doing a half-gainer off the branch and tumbling ass over teakettle forty feet down, only to land with a loud splash and then to sink beneath the surface as if he had never existed.

Walks were never the same after that. I missed my daily raccoon interlude.

## Chapter 7

# Winter Wonderland

*Historic Lows. Once in a Lifetime Wind Chills.* Yawn. I turned off the TV when the hyperbole reached ridiculous heights. I knew better. It was worse in the 1960s and 70s. And, back then, they didn't bother to cancel all the schools or close the grocery stores or stop mail delivery. Nope. My brother and I stood every frigid morning at the end of the driveway, waiting for the school bus, which was freezing inside as well. *It's January, for God's sake!* I thought after I turned off the hype on TV. *In Minnesota. We have antifreeze in our veins!* Or at least we used to. Now, we seem to fall completely apart when the temperature approaches anything below twenty degrees. And if it snows, even a dusting? It's *Breaking News!* fodder for all the news shows and hysteria reigns across the land.

Okay, fine. Let's say it's thirty below, along with a nice, brisk breeze. As long as you wear tons of layers and cover your exposed skin, you will be fine. Unless you decide to trip and fall face first in the snow and neglect to get up anytime soon. Then, you will turn into a human popsicle. Remember not to fall, and you should be fine.

Or if you do fall, do your damnedest to get back up! Earlier today, I went outside for a few minutes clad only in a fleece jacket, fuzzy owl slippers, and pajamas. I seem to have made it back inside alive.

I have to admit…I did fall for the hype and hyperbole leading up to this particular *Once in a Lifetime* event and decided I had better close up the garage window so my mini horses, Misty and Sunny, and Donald, the goat, wouldn't get too cold since the prevailing blustery winds come from that direction. Yes, I know they're supposed to be accustomed to living in the great outdoors, no matter the weather. Doesn't matter to me—I want them *comfortable.*

One of the panes of glass in their garage had broken a few months before, and after cleaning up everything so they wouldn't step in any broken glass, I hadn't bothered to fix it. That broken pane was on the northwest side—where the coldest winds come screaming in.

Once I figured out the supplies I would need, I had to make a special run to Menard's for heavy-weight plastic sheeting, wooden shims, and wood screws. Choosing the screws was the most aggravating part. Why are there 10,000 versions of screws in 15,000 different lengths? Pointy. Not-so-pointy. Totally-not-pointy. Those are called bolts, by the way, not screws. My head was spinning, but I made it through somehow.

I grabbed a cordless drill from the house and brought all the items into the garage and set them down. Donald immediately leaped in to "help" me. First, he chewed on the wood shims. He must have been dreaming of summer when he could chew on the buckthorn branches. After snatching countless shims away from him, I gave up and let him have his fun—wood is wood. I made sure the shims didn't have any type of preservative on them before he chewed.

Next, as I rolled out the length of plastic I would need, he stepped on it and slid around before trying to, yes, eat it. I shooed him away and told him to go eat hay with the minis. Eventually, he got the hint after I yelled at him several times.

Sunny, Donald, and Misty enjoying the snow.

It took forever and countless dropped screws and lots of swearing, but the plastic was now secure, and the window was covered. But I wasn't done in my mission to keep my minis and goat warm.

I had an unused chicken brooder lamp and, along with a 150-watt heat bulb, it would make it feel like they were standing under a warm summer sun. Trust me, they loved it. I didn't use the 250-watt version because my electric bill would go through the roof with those babies. I'd learned that from using them in the chicken coop. Now, I had to grab a ladder and figure out a way to secure the light to the overhead joist so there would be no chance it would come loose and fall on to the floor, or that Donald could reach it and burn himself. I kicked all the straw away to be sure of no fire worries, although, with how well I'd tied that sucker up, I didn't think there was any danger. As soon as I turned it on, Misty and Sunny imme-diately came and stood under it. The minis wouldn't share their spot with the goat, and I had to make another trip to town, this time to the feed store, to buy another brooder lamp for him. Meanwhile, I was getting colder and colder. I ended up standing under the heat lamp myself for a while.

Breezy can't take having the cold snow on her front paws, and my next trip was to Chuck and Don's, a local pet supply store, where they fitted her with stylish boots. She strutted the runway in the store (otherwise known as an aisle) to cooing from the employees. She walked like a duck, but she kind of liked them, especially when everybody told her how cute she looked. Once I got home, I realized I should have had them train me how to put them on her. It's worst first thing in the morning when I'm not anywhere near awake, and she's dancing around needing to get outside *now*. Somehow, she stands patiently on three legs as I fumble around, pushing them onto her paws and fumbling with the velcro closures. Bleary-eyed, at one point, I looked up to see Nutter, her secret cat boyfriend, standing under Breezy's elbow, holding up her leg so I could finish putting the boot on her front paw. I burst out laughing. It reminded me of when the farrier comes out to trim the minis' hooves—she has a contraption that looks like a small stool and places the horse's knee onto it to stabilize them as she works. Nutter figured out how to do that all by himself. It took me forever to put the other boots on since I was still cackling loudly.

It's bad enough that I shamelessly spoil my dog, cats, chickens, mini horses, and goat. I guess I tend to think of it in terms of how I would feel if it was me out there in the blustery cold, and then I decide, *Why not make life easier and more comfortable for them?* I invariably forget to add, *While making life far more complicated for me.*

Yeah. Except now I'm doing it for the wild animals, too.

It all started a couple of years ago, on April 14—a day that will live on in infamy. A huge blizzard had started late the day before but really got going by Saturday morning. Thunder cracked and boomed in the afternoon. It's rare to have thundersnow. When you get thunder during a snowstorm, it's a bad one. Winds gusted over 50 mph, and a tree snapped and fell in the wind.

I drove to town in the morning to stock up on bird food and hay before the storm got too bad. The snow was coming down heavily when I got home. Breezy helped me do things outside for a while but then wanted to go inside where it was warm; she was covered with snow. I filled the bird feeders while frantic chickadees flitted and chirped in the nearby birch tree. Done with that task, I then sat on the raised brick flowerbed by the front door, snug in my parka, and watched them dig in. The snow was coming down and being blown sideways by the wind, and yet it felt peaceful out there. I love sitting outside in the silence of a snowstorm. My perch next to the house was somewhat sheltered, and bundled up in my thick parka, I wasn't cold. I went inside after about fifteen minutes.

Being that it was now April, it supposedly was spring, but that day, winter clawed back with a vengeance. I relished the return of winter's quiet—snow pattering down, birds nearly silent. Days before, spring had been in full swing. All the migrating birds had arrived: geese were honking, ducks quacking, gulls wheeling high above on their migration north, the robins were ebullient. Spring is *noisy.*

Later that day, more booming thunder. The windows shook, and the thunder made Nutter jump in alarm in his cat bed in the bay window.

A few hours later, I was back outside with Breezy to refill the feeders and feed the minis and Donald. Suddenly, a huge crack of thunder boomed; it went on forever. I jumped, then smiled and laughed in delight. Breezy went back inside while I again sat on the planter with my feet up, feeling happy. I was bundled in my parka with the hood on my head while the snow pelted down mercilessly, already covering my tracks to the bird feeder in mere minutes.

A large shape winged in and alighted on the pine tree at the edge of the yard. A barred owl was watching the birds at the feeder with interest. I eventually walked over there, five inches of snow soon

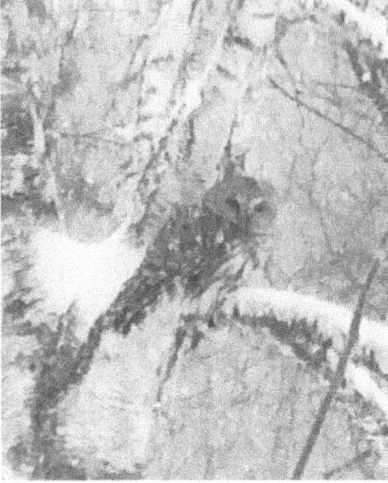

A barred owl.

filling my tennis shoes. I'm not sure why the heck I hadn't put on boots.

"Could you maybe hunt somewhere else?" I asked it. "I'd hate it if you ate these birds." She stared at me, unafraid, listening as I blathered on. A few minutes later, she flew deep into the woods. Did she understand me? Maybe. But the birds were safe, and that's all that mattered. I slogged back through the snow and went inside to snuggle with Breezy.

Eventually, eighteen inches of snow fell. It was a brutal slap in the face.

Each day, the birds were frantic, searching for food. With the drifts of snow covering everything, they had nothing to eat. I bought more birdfeed, raisins, bread, and cracked corn. I tried to think of what all the different kinds of birds might eat: robins like fruit and worms; the other birds eat seed or suet. Crows eat just about everything. I dug through the freezer and found long-forgotten packages of frozen berries for the robins. For the crows, I found meat that had been in the freezer for a while and was far beyond its expiration date. In all the years I've lived here, I've been trying to get the crows to trust me. When I offered them the freezer-burned meat, it was the first time the crows came to eat, although they'd been observing me from their high perches for years. I know most people detest crows, but I've always loved them. I'm not sure why. Maybe because everyone else loathed them and, early in my life, I decided somebody needed to love them, and that person was me.

Early one morning, a hen turkey was at the bird feeder, digging in the snow for seeds. She saw me watching her from the window.

She wandered off, and I opened the door to go out and fill the feeders and scatter seeds on the snow. Two Canada geese were now at the feeder.

They had never come near the house because of Breezy. I couldn't imagine how they were surviving. The ponds were still frozen solid with thick ice, the grass was covered with eighteen inches of snow, with nothing anywhere for them to eat. I brought out the birdseed in an ice cream bucket, and they let me cautiously approach the feeders. The male hissed, his sinuous neck undulating like a cobra. The female came closer as I neared them. I was a little scared because they are large, strong birds, and I didn't want to get attacked. It was like they were begging me for food. *Come on, you have to feed us! We'll starve otherwise.* I scattered birdseed on the snow and backed away as they gobbled it up.

Later, the mallard ducks came to eat the cracked corn I had poured out onto the driveway near the mini horse pen. The crows now come every morning. A raccoon even showed up at noon one day for food. I guess word had gotten around about the free chow at my house. To make it easier on all the critters to find the corn, I shoveled the snow on the driveway down to the asphalt and scattered the corn in several piles. Then, I shoveled a trail for the birds to walk to the next pile so they didn't have to struggle through the snow. At least I'm getting my exercise.

It's kind of embarrassing because I know the park employees can see me when their trucks go in and out to their maintenance facility across the road. Their driveway is about 500 feet away from my house through the trees

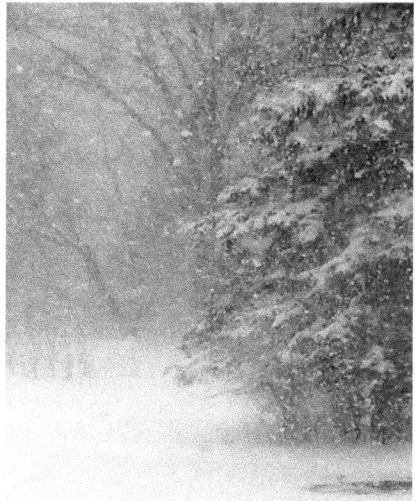

An April blizzard in Minnesota. Yuck.

and across the front pond; not that far at all. They see me in dawn's first light, mindlessly shoveling snow in the middle of nowhere and pouring corn from a bucket, wearing my old airline parka and bright flannel pajamas and boots. Sometimes the trucks sit there for a long time, windshields pointed in my direction. They probably have binoculars trained on me by this point. *There! Look! She's doing it again. What the hell is she doing?* One worker will say to the other. The other worker no doubt replies to his buddy, *Wow. That's really weird, isn't it?* The first worker then turns to the other and says deadpan, *Yup. That's putting it mildly.* And they drive away.

Since it was mid-April, the snow melted quickly, and within five days. the grass was peeking up here and there through the remaining mounds of snow. All the various critters now had something to eat and they didn't need to depend on me to feed them. The mallard couple that's been coming to my yard for several years stopped by and went for a swim in the small area of thawed ice in the front garden pond. Spring had finally sprung and life was good.

My neighbor, Bill, is a true animal whisperer, even more than me. The turkeys peck around on his front steps and look through his front door. Flocks of geese hang out in his front yard, going back and forth to the pond across the road. They have it so good there that, one December, after the ponds had all frozen solid and the geese should have been long gone on their migration, a hardened few were still hanging out waiting for their handout after all their relatives had headed south for the winter. The turkeys at my house had never warmed up to me at that point, and I wondered why they liked Bill better than me. It was more than likely the same flock since they head through my pasture going in his direction. I decided it was time to befriend me some turkeys using my secret weapon, cracked corn. It worked better than I had ever envisioned. Now I can't get rid of them.

## Chapter 8

# Ssssomething Sssslithers in the Night

Late one August afternoon, I walked with Breezy on her leash to the end of the driveway to get the mail. A boy on a bike was riding circles on the gravel road. He was maybe ten years old. You never see kids out and about alone anymore. Parents keep them on a much tighter leash than when I was a kid. My mom used to tell my brother and me, "Why don't you two go and play on the road for a while?" Seriously. She said exactly that: "Go play on the road." We were driving her nuts. Back then, the few cars on our dirt road were invariably neighbors, and they watched out for us so it was safe enough.

I said hi to the boy and went over to the mailbox. I pulled open the door to see one lousy piece of junk mail. It almost wasn't worth the walk up to the end of the driveway.

He rode up on his bike and asked, "Are the yellow and black snakes poisonous?"

I knew right away what kind he meant. "No, that's a garter snake. They're okay, but I have been bit when I tried to pick one up." I flashed back to when I was his age, and my family was up north at the cabin. I was walking on the path back from my friend Anita's cabin and saw a snake lounging in the dappled sun. I leaned down to pick it up—don't ask me why—but before I could grab it, the snake launched itself up at my hand and clamped down on my index finger. I never knew snakes had teeth. They do. Sharp ones. And it hurt like mad. I flapped my hand back and forth until it finally let go and slithered away into the grass. I ran to where my parents were sitting on Adirondack chairs overlooking the lake and drinking beer and told them what had happened. "Snakes don't bite! You have a vivid imagination," my parents said, even when I showed them the two puncture wounds on my finger. They didn't believe me. They usually didn't.

I brought my attention back to the present and the boy on the road. He turned his bike and pointed about twenty feet away. "A snake got run over right there."

I took Breezy over for a look. Ugh. The snake was belly up, and its intestines were on the outside. It was a teenage snake—not fully grown.

"Poor thing," I said.

"Yeah," the boy replied. "I hate when people run over stuff. Can't they see it?"

I agreed with him as I glanced back down at the poor snake. When I'm driving on our dirt road, I always pull over and wait for whatever critter happens to be crossing the road. Oftentimes, I get out to help turtles across because they tend to pull their head into their shells, hunker down, and sit there. Except for the full-grown snapping turtles. I don't help them. Those guys are on their own.

"I suppose I could move it so it doesn't get run over more." I looked at my junk mail. "I don't care if I get guts on this." I leaned down and slid the mail under the snake so I could pick it up and move it to the weeds at the side of the road for "burial."

It writhed. I screamed and jumped back. "*Omigod. It's still alive.* Yuck! How can it still be alive? Gross. Gross. *Gross.*"

The boy looked down at the snake and back to me. I didn't want to act like a total wimp in front of him, so I pulled myself together somehow without barfing all over the place.

"Well, that's that," I told the kid. "No way am I going to move it if it's still alive. It would make its pain even worse. We need someone in a car to come and run it over again and put it out of its misery, and your bike tire won't do the job. I guess we'll have to leave it."

"Guess so," he replied with a glum expression, looking again at the snake.

"Well…it was nice to meet you anyway!" I said and turned to walk with Breezy back to my driveway as the boy pedaled off on his bike down the road.

I'm not one of those people who scream bloody murder when I see a snake. And I don't hate them with a nameless passion, either. When I see one, I usually let it do its thing. Unless it's trying to eat one of the little tree frogs or toads—then I leap into action. Several times over the years, I've been sitting on the front steps, hanging out, when I hear a high-pitched squealing. Running to investigate on one of those occasions, I found a snake with a small green tree frog firmly clamped in its maw. What was weird was that the snake was on the side of the garage—as in four or five feet up and hanging on to the wood siding. I'd never seen a snake do something like that. How was he holding on? It's not like he had hands or feet. The tiny frog was screaming in terror. I couldn't let him die. I had to save his little green butt!

"Leave him alone, snake! Drop him! You are not going to kill him if I have anything to say about it." The snake turned to face me, frog still struggling in his mouth. Its reptilian eyes coldly appraised me and, dismissing me, it turned away to finish its breakfast. That pissed me off—a snake dissing me—so I grabbed the nearest thing I could find, a small branch, and poked at the snake. It writhed in anger, and I was worried it was going to go after me. It was a big garter snake. I backed away a few feet, and tried again. The snake fell from the siding and dropped the frog, which darted under a bush. The snake turned its attention to me. I had single-handedly taken away its breakfast, and it wasn't happy. I felt kind of bad about it, but I couldn't let a sweet little frog die in terror like that. We had a lengthy stare-down, and it slithered off into the grass in defeat.

Another time, it was my favorite toad being consumed by another snake. This toad was the biggest, fattest toad I'd ever seen. It hung out near the front patio, and I'd see it every so often. It seemed to be friendly enough, for a toad. Toads make a beautiful trilling noise, and it always puts a smile on my face. They may be homely, but they sure can sing. That day, I heard the trilling, but it was more of a screech. I ran over to the birch tree where the noise seemed to be coming from. Once again, I saw a large snake busily chomping down on something. I realized it was my favorite toad when I saw its rear legs sticking out of the snake's wide-open jaw. The rest of it was already inside.

I didn't know if I could save him; he looked like he was too far in the snake's mouth. I got right down in that snake's face and snarled, "You are eating my toad buddy. That is *not* going to happen. Let him go *right now.*" The snake curled up into a coil and glared at me, toad legs kicking the whole time. "I mean it. Let him go. He's my favorite toad. Find something else to eat."

I grabbed another stick and poked at the snake repeatedly. Eventually he got sick of it and opened his mouth, probably to attack me or hiss or whatever the hell snakes do when they're pissed. I redoubled my attack, because he had dropped the toad when he turned his attention to me.

"Run, toad! Run!" I yelled. I guess toads don't really run, they hop, but the little guy heard me and beat cheeks out of there. Meanwhile, the snake had slithered into the hosta garden.

I saw the toad several times after that. I'm not sure if he really knew that I had saved his life, but I did—which is all that really matters.

Seeing a snake in the great outdoors is one thing because it's normal and nothing to be concerned about. "Outdoors" is the operative word.

One evening in late November, I had arrived home after attending my friend Pam's sixtieth birthday party. Happy to be home, I snuggled into my recliner, a fuzzy throw over my lap, a book at hand ready to be opened and delved into. *What was that noise?* It sounded like my cat, Felix, was having a seizure in the dining room. I looked over and saw him flopping around under the kitchen table. *Oh my God. What's wrong with him?* I wondered as I launched myself out of the chair and ran into the other room. He was only four months old; how could there be anything wrong with him?

I knelt down next to him and realized he had been stalking prey—which turned out to be a Three. Stinking. Foot. Long. Snake.

I pushed Felix out of the way and looked down at it curled up under the table. I had only had one beer at the party. I certainly couldn't be drunk or hallucinating, could I? Was that really a snake? In my *house?* At the end of freaking *November?* Yes. It was.

Felix, all grown up.

I rocked back onto my heels while I quietly had a nervous break-down. I don't mind snakes outside—that's fine. But a snake in the house? Meanwhile, the snake had uncoiled and gone to hide under the baseboard heat register, then poked its head out and stretched itself along the top. Yuck.

Great. How was I going to get it out of there? Every time I moved toward it, the snake disappeared back into the register. No way was I letting that thing wander around at night while I was in bed. I wondered—how did he get in the house? He had to have been in one of the flowerpots I brought inside to overwinter some of my plants. The last one I had brought in was a huge geranium and that was a month prior. This thing had been hiding in my house *for a month.*

*Oh. My. God.*

I grabbed a chair and sat down to think about what to do. How could I catch it? What would I do with it if I actually *did* catch it? As I pondered, all I could think about was that this kind of stuff only happens to me. The weirder the thing, the more likely it will include me in some way. As I thought this, the snake poked its head up, its tongue tasting the air.

I was going to try to do the hook maneuver you see when people catch rattlesnakes, but I didn't have a metal coat hanger, so I figured that option was out. Digging around the house, I found a fly swatter that had an open metal end that I could use in lieu of the coat hanger.

The snake had reappeared and was now slithering along the top of the heat register, so I darted over and was somehow able to loop the metal end over its head. Before I could lift the snake up and out, it yanked itself backward out of my snare and hid again underneath the register.

In a panic, I ran around the house trying to find something to put him in if I could somehow get him to emerge on the floor again. I found an old clear plastic container that my mom had stored photos of our family from the 1960s. I dumped them out onto the floor and ran back to the dining room holding the container.

*He was gone. Shit!* Where did he go? Was he still close by, or had he ventured elsewhere in the house—like my *bedroom?* I grabbed a flashlight and got down on my hands and knees on the floor to look for him. No luck. I didn't see his beady little eyes anywhere under the registers.

I sat in a chair, hyperventilating and freaking out. I envisioned staying up all night in that chair because I didn't want to wake up in the middle of the night in bed with him under the covers next to me. I could picture his little head popping up on the pillow next to me as I lay in bed. As I waited for him to reappear, I wished I had some booze in the house. You never have it when you *really* need it. Time passed, and the snake surfaced once again from the heat register and looked around, but when he saw me, back down into the register he went and hid again. This went on for at least twenty minutes. I sat in my chair and pleaded with him to come out. "Come on, guy. I need to go to bed. I'm old. I can't stay up late anymore. Get your butt out here so I can catch you."

I had found a pair of heavy leather gloves in one of the closets so that if I had to pick him up with my hands, he wouldn't be able to

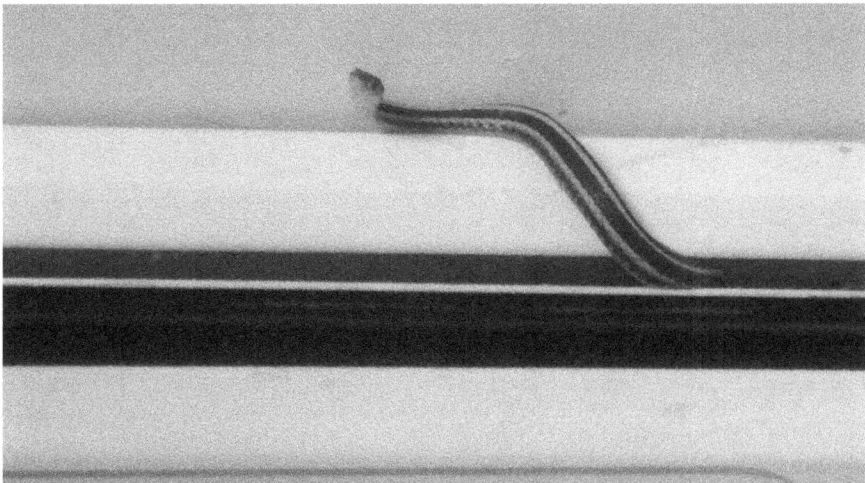

The snake coming out of the heat register.
Yes—it was just as disgusting as it looks.

bite through them. I remembered how much it had hurt when that snake had bitten me when I was a kid.

He came up and stretched out along the top of the heat register, a truly creepy thing to witness. I sat in my chair in despair and watched the snake doing snake things *inside my house.* The situation was so surreal I really felt like I had gone nuts. How was I going to tell my friends about this? Was I even *going* to tell them about this? They would think I was hallucinating. Or nuts. Or both.

When the snake decided to make a break for it and looked like he was heading to the floor, I finally had had enough and went into the living room and grabbed Nutter, my fourteen-year-old cat, who was sound asleep. I brought him into the other room, set him down, pointed at the snake, and said, "*Get him!*" When the snake made its way on to the floor, I pushed Nutter at him. Nice mom, sacrificing my kitty. The cat didn't notice the damn thing, even when he stepped right on top of it. Nutter walked on it a couple times as the snake curled up into a ball. Seeing my chance, I grabbed the plastic container, pushed Nutter out of danger, and dropped it on top of the snake, finally trapping it. It was *so* mad—baring its fangs and striking

Trapped inside the plastic container with duct
tape around the edges keeping it secure.

with lightning-like swiftness at the clear sides. That sucker would have put a world of hurt on me right about then if it had been able to get at me.

I had to figure out how to get something underneath the container so I could lift it all without the snake being able to escape. I tore the house apart for the second time that night and finally found a thin piece of stiff cardboard from a picture frame that was the right size. I slipped it underneath and duct taped it all around the container bottom as the snake punched with its head at the sides in attack. When the cardboard was securely fastened, I felt reasonably sure the snake wouldn't be able to get out in the middle of the night.

I carried the whole thing down to the basement, the snake striking at the sides the whole time, put the container on top of the washing machine, shut off the light, and made doubly sure the door leading upstairs was securely closed. When I finally went to bed, I shut the bedroom door, which I never do, and I prayed the snake didn't get out while I was sleeping. It was a long night.

It had to have been crawling around the house for a month, yet I had never seen it. As far as what it could have been eating, tons of mice were available, even when the cats bothered to hunt them.

The next morning, when I got up, I was hoping it had all been a really bad dream. I didn't want to go downstairs to see if it had truly happened and if the snake really was there. What was I going to do with it? It needed to go outside, but it was the end of November. How would it survive? It needed to find a place to hibernate, stat. And then I remembered where the snakes lived—the steps outside the back patio had a hole on the side that led under the porch. I'd seen snakes coming in and out of there for years. That was where I would let my snake go.

I waited until early afternoon. The temperature was only in the low forties, but by afternoon, the sun had warmed the patio pavers and the back step. The fact that I wasn't looking forward in the least to doing this certainly didn't factor into the delay in retrieving the snake from downstairs.

Opening the basement door, I turned on the light and looked over at the washing machine. Yup. It was true. It all really did happen. The snake was glaring at me from inside his container. It was time. I carried the container outside to the back of the house and set it on the ground next to the step as I gathered my courage. I wasn't sure how this was all going to go down.

First, I gave the snake a pep talk. "Okay, here's how it's going to work. I'm going to take the tape off, and I'll flip the container on its side and let you go. Try not to bite me, okay? I'm not really in the mood to be bitten." The snake had settled down and was looking around. The last time he'd been outside, there had probably been leaves on the trees and green grass. That wasn't the case any longer; a coating of snow was layered on the now-dormant grass, and the trees were bare.

I removed the tape, slid the cardboard from under the container, flipped it on its side, and unceremoniously dumped the snake onto the patio. I pointed to the hole next to the step leading under the porch. "See that? It's where you need to go. If you stay out here, you'll freeze solid. You need to get your butt under there ASAP. All the snakes live in there, so you'll have some new friends. Now get going."

As I stood up, the snake looked up at me with what may have been a quizzical expression, like he was wondering why I was being nice. People aren't usually nice to snakes; in fact, they're downright evil to them. I was obviously acting out of character for a human. I picked up the container, cardboard, and tape and went back into the house. I checked back a few hours later and the snake was gone. I'm hoping he figured out to go into the hole so he'd be safe, although I'll never know for sure.

## Chapter 9

# Code Not Compliant

The city sent out a letter warning me they were coming to our neighborhood to do "Code Inspections." Seriously? We live in the country, on a dead-end dirt road where nothing much has changed since my family built this house in 1963. Why would the city feel the need? It's not like any of the neighbors can see each other and complain about their yards. Nor would we. We're kind of throwbacks to a simpler time—live and let live, with an I-don't-give-a-damn-what-you're-doing-over-there-as-long-as-it-doesn't-impact-me kind of attitude about life. That attitude is obvious, considering no one has ever mentioned hearing some of the noises (and swear words) that have come from my neck of the woods as I yelled at the coyotes.

The code inspection handout said that all weeds eight inches and higher must be removed. Well, great. That would mean I'd need to remove over fifteen acres of weeds. That ain't gonna happen. Perhaps the city officials are unaware that it's called a *pasture*. Perhaps my little town is getting a bit too full of itself and is thinking we are now actually a big-time suburb.

"Garbage cans must be in an enclosed area." Do you think putting them between two oak trees would qualify? Otherwise, I'd have to lug those two heavy things all the way up the tenth-of-a-mile driveway each week, then lug them right back down a day later. You betcha. I can hardly wait for ten inches of snow to fall so I can slog through it dragging those things. I can barely pull them twenty feet.

Oh, and what is this? "House number must be large enough to be read from the street." Wow. That means the numbers will each need to be fifteen feet tall! And I'd need to remove about thirty trees. I'll get right on it. I've got me a circular saw and some plywood to make me some signs. Yup. I'll get 'er done. Then I'll spray paint those suckers hot pink. That will fulfill the other requirement—that they "stand out from the background," which is a brown house and green everything else. Eight-inch-tall weeds, remember?

Uh oh. "No outside storage of any debris." I am *soooo* screwed. Especially if they find the 1960s-era dump my dad made down a steep hill out by the pasture. I worked to clean up what was left of the dump a few years ago, but it was difficult since it is on a massively steep incline full of sticker bushes. I valiantly attempted to emulate a mountain goat as I pulled things up the hill, then eventually gave up on the last few items and dragged myself up to the top by grabbing onto nearby bushes, dusted myself off, and went to get an ice-cold beverage.

"Woodpiles must be stacked in a neat, safe, and orderly fashion." Yeah, okay. I'll get right on that, too. Although, my trusty electric chainsaw will have a tough time with the four-foot-wide oak trunks lying haphazardly here and there and pretty damn much every-where. Unfortunately, I may not have enough extension cords to reach the back forty, since I ran over a nice long cord the other day while mowing. It made quite the mess. Luckily, I was able to extri-cate it from the mower blades, so I didn't need to call my brother to confess I'd run over something once again, and could he please come remove whatever it was this time?

Then I looked on the city website, and I think they will be citing me for the mini horses being in the garage as it isn't one hundred feet away from my house. That's unfortunate, because I can't put them in the pasture. I have no way to fix the fencing, and in any case, they, and for certain the goat, would attract the coyotes for a nice all-you-can-eat buffet. Plus, they would all get loose and rampage through the neighborhood like they used to, and the fun would commence.

Ahh...the manure. Yes. Let's talk about the manure, shall we? Crap. (Oh! I made a bit of a pun!) No way am I getting out of that code violation unless I can get the neighbor down here with his skid loader in the next week or two before the city shows up. Then where can I hide the copious piles? Ah yes...behind the eight-inch-high weeds!

If the city worker goes up to the pole barn, they will see the dilapidated little garage that is falling down around my sister-in-law's '55 Chevy, which has been rotting away inside for at least thirty-five years. Would that be considered a junked or inoperable vehicle? I kind of think so, considering the registration tabs on the license plate say 1981. And I'm not sure if they will spot the 1939 Case tractor hiding in the trees behind the pole barn. That's definitely an inoperable vehicle and has been for about forty years...maybe closer to fifty.

At least I am in compliance with the allowable number of cats and dogs. For once. Not sure about the chickens though, especially since I have roosters—the city frowns on roosters. But since I am zoned agricultural, I think I can get away with it. Oh, this will be so much fun!

## Chapter 10

# What's Good for the Goose
# is Good for the Gander

It's hard for me to tell the various wild critters apart. Deer have small variations in coloring, and the ducks, turkeys, geese, and other birds' feathers may have slightly different patterns. I've learned to identify some of the individuals based on their behavior when they're around me. Like the Canada goose couple that nest each year in a pond a short distance down my dirt road.

In that area, two ponds border the road on each side, and there's a narrow strip of grass between the ponds and road. Each day, I'd see the two geese hanging out there. They arrived each year in late March or early April from their winter stomping grounds. It seems like the geese (and ducks) choose the same ponds each year and chase off any interlopers to their chosen territory. Every day I would stop my car and roll down the window to say hi and check on how they were doing. The male goose was a handsome guy with warm, expressive eyes. He was friendly as long as his wife wasn't nearby;

then, he would hiss and try to chase me away. His wife was not friendly in the least. I kind of wondered what he saw in her.

The first year, the two geese swam in the ponds and sat each day at the edge of the road but I didn't notice any nesting behavior. The next year, they built a nest in the smaller pond. I drove past one day, and spied Mrs. Goose sitting atop the nest she'd built on top of the muskrat house a short distance out in the pond. It was a great location—surrounded by water so it was safe from predators like coyotes or raccoons, and yet sheltered by tall grasses and small swamp-dwelling trees. She sat on the nest day in and day out—rain, snow, or sun—she was there on her nest. Her husband, Mr. Handsome, swam alone in the pond across the road, whiling away the hours and days until their brood was born. I could hardly wait to see the little babies.

The few times when his wife was off her nest and hanging out near him on the road, I drove past and didn't stop because I knew I wouldn't get a good reception. Whenever he was alone, however, I pulled over and talked to him. "Hi, handsome. How's everything going? It looks like your wife is doing a good job over there. You

Mrs. Goose on her nest in the pond.

Mr. Goose sitting on the roadside waiting patiently for his wife.

must get bored here, all by yourself the whole day. Well, at least *you* like me. Your wife can't stand me. Okay…have a good day!" Mr. Handsome listened patiently as I blathered on and on. He had the most gorgeous eyes and, for a goose, a really calm, Zen personality. His wife, on the other hand, was kind of a snot. And here I was, sitting in my car, talking to a goose like it could understand me.

That first year, the rains came down non-stop, and the water in the ponds rose inexorably. I'm no expert, but it seemed like the eggs were taking forever to hatch. All the other geese had already had their babies, and tiny, fluffy goslings were everywhere. All except for Mr. and Mrs. Goose.

I drove past one day on my way into town to see the two of them on the side of the road, looking forlorn. She had abandoned her nest. When I came home later, the two of them were out in the pond on a hummock of swamp grass, standing solemnly in front of the eggs in the nest. I stopped the car for a moment to watch them. I swear to God they were grieving and saying goodbye to their unborn children. I cried as I sat there watching because it truly seemed to be a funeral ceremony.

Fast forward to the next spring. It was late March, and most of the ice was still on the ponds; only small areas had melted and were free of ice. A long, cold, snowy winter was nearly done. I drove home after a long day at my job. In the distance, I noticed two geese walking across the road in front of me to the small pond. As I passed by, I looked over, and yes, it was them—the goose couple was back! They must have flown in that day. I stopped and rolled down my window, and said to the male, "You're back! You're here!" I pulled up near the female, and she flew the short distance to where her nest had been the previous year and inspected the spot. The water in the pond was higher than it had been in decades because of the vast amounts of snow that winter, and I wondered if she would be able to nest there again.

She did build her nest in the same location, but once again, the rains were relentless, and soon, the nest and eggs were completely inundated and covered by water. For the second year in a row, she had to abandon her nest. I watched each day as the tableau unfolded and felt so bad for them again.

The third year when they returned, they didn't even bother trying to nest in that spot again. I saw them standing in their usual place on the side of the road when they first returned in the spring, but then they disappeared. They must have found a new place to nest. I do miss seeing that handsome guy. But his wife—not so much.

I truly believe animals possess a spiritual sense, even before I saw the geese praying over their failed nest. I can describe what I saw them doing that day in no other way: they had lowered their heads as they stood in front of their failed nest and were grieving.

I read an article once in the Minneapolis newspaper—at one of the lakes near downtown, a man was walking on the path around the lake. In the distance, he noticed a dead crow lying on the ground. A flock of crows was gathered in a circle around the dead crow. He stopped to observe and realized that one crow was the "leader," and he watched as it placed a twig from its beak onto the ground near the dead crow. He was shocked to realize that the crows were holding a ceremony resembling a funeral.

Recently online, I read another article that included a photo of a cat dead in the road, with turkeys doing a circular dance around its body. The person who wrote the article thought it was macabre and creepy. I thought they were simply honoring its life.

Just because animals don't "talk" the way we humans do doesn't mean they don't communicate and have full lives, not so unlike our own. Sure—they don't drive cars, text unmercifully on smartphones, etc. I'd say that not being addicted to smartphones actually makes them a lot smarter than us.

You learn so much about the natural world by observing animals and paying attention. If you sit quietly outside, close your eyes, and simply listen, you might hear chickadees calling, turkey gobbling, blue jays screeching, and crows making all kinds of racket. That doesn't seem out of the ordinary, but when all the birds burst out at once, it usually means there's a raptor or other predator somewhere nearby. I never knew that—I thought the birds were simply being noisy and irritating. No, there is a method to their madness, and the different types of birds all pay attention to each other. When one spots a predator and raises the alarm, they all know it. My chickens also listen to the wild birds and cock their heads to look up into the sky to see if any hawks or owls are incoming. I've noticed that the squirrels and deer also listen to the birds. If deer are in my yard and hear the birds freaking out, they keep a wary eye out because it could mean a coyote is coming their way.

I've found over the years that paying attention to nature has taught me not only about animals but also about people. How people interact with each other, both good and bad, is similar in so many ways to the animal interactions I've observed.

Animals bully each other just like people do to one another.

For a time, four young male turkeys were hanging out together and coming to my bird feeders. I suppose their mom had kicked all her kids out of the flock when they got old enough, and they dispersed to find an area to claim as their own. These four particular turkeys warmed up to me eventually since they knew I was the one doling out the gravy train. One of them was smaller than the others and was lowest on the pecking order. He was submissive, and they chased him from one corn pile to another, refusing to let him have any. And he let them do it. I felt sorry for him. They were complete jerks. I was outside one morning, and it happened again. I shouted to the three bullying him, "Hey! Leave him alone!" I turned to the timid little guy and said, "Stand your ground! What's the worst they can do to you? Peck you? Big deal. Peck them back!" Of course, my little pep talk with a wild turkey did absolutely nothing to change the dynamic, but it made me feel better.

Breezy and I went on a walk one hot summer evening. We meandered down the road, turned into the park, and continued onto a winding trail through towering oaks. A huge pileated woodpecker landed on a dead tree to our left, allowed us to approach, and let us stand directly below. It was only fifteen feet above us. These are normally very shy birds. It calmly looked down at us as it ate some type of insect from a knot in the tree. It was a magical moment. I have no idea if some sort of higher message was in this interaction; I was simply happy to have been a part of it. Opening myself to moments like this brings me joy and peace. I just need to slow down enough to recognize and notice them.

# Chapter 11

# Stalking the Wild Coyote

I tend to scream a lot when I'm outside—it seems to be a reflex at this point. It's not the mean, yelling kind of scream, although I've been known to do that from time to time. It's more the, "Oh, dear God, what is that thing, and is it going to try to eat me?" kind of scream. The panic-stricken-reptilian-survival-part-of-the-brain engages.

The neighbors must be used to it after all these years. I imagine they turn to each other: "What was that?" "Oh, probably just Sue. She does that every so often." "Wonder why?" "Who knows." It's funny, though—I have never heard any of the other neighbors scream or swear at coyotes. Although I have heard a rifle shot a time or two, target-shooting coyotes. That neighbor is smart. He doesn't warn them—he blasts them.

Oh—and this is classic. Case in point: I had barely typed these words when an unholy caterwauling howl arose across the back pond. It must have been about twenty coyotes, yipping and howling and screeching. They have impeccable timing; I'll say that for the mangy bastards.

As I was saying before I was so rudely interrupted, I barely hear the neighbors. They might call for their dogs every once in awhile, although, come to think of it, when the next-door neighbor's dogs went wild the other night at dusk, presumably because a coyote trotted past their yard, I swear I heard her say, "Go get 'em!" I must be rubbing off. Next thing you know, she'll be seen at the sporting goods store, loading up on baseball bats to brain them with.

Perhaps the number of coyotes coming to my house has something to do with the yard being rather—how do I put it delicately—wild? As though nature is encroaching, and is about to wrest complete and final control, and I'm powerless to stop it. My trusty little electric chainsaw and I are no match.

The new neighbors in the McMansion at the top of the back hill called me one afternoon. "We've been clearing the brush around here."

I replied, "I hear the chainsaw sometimes."

"Pretty quiet on your end," he said.

"Well, yeah, until I yell at the coyotes. You had to have heard me do *that!*"

He wisely changed the subject.

Coyotes had begun appearing again for the first time in over two years. For some reason they lay low for a couple years, and soon enough, I see them everywhere again. Breezy had been acting really jumpy. When the dry oak leaves skittered across the patio from the wind, she immediately twirled and jumped straight upward. She knew the damn coyotes were gunning for her. Every night, there had been tons of howling and yipping, which drove her into a frenzy of barking. Trying to calm her down, I told her that if she barks, they'll know they're getting to her...so don't let them know. Having said that, I turned away to open the window and yelled at the bastards. Guess that means they know they're getting to me, too. Maybe I should take my own advice.

One afternoon, I noticed a coyote in my backyard run into the woods, and it headed for the trail to my brother's house. I texted my niece to let her know it was coming her way and to make sure her dog was safe. Good thing, too, because when she put Jade inside, she saw the coyote coming toward her house. Next day, two more coyotes ran through my backyard at 2:30 p.m. on a bright, sunny day. I used to think they were only active at night. I've since learned through hard-won experience that isn't true—they hunt whenever they damn well want. Who's going to stop them? They're the apex predator around here.

Soon enough, I noticed a young male coming to visit us at all hours. Early one morning, Breezy was out for her morning constitutional, sniffing around the yard and checking the perimeter for threats. I was pulling weeds near the front patio just for the heck of it, although it was a rather futile effort. I noticed Breezy on alert near the woods by the front pond. Her ears were up, hackles raised, and she was looking into the woods. I called for her to come, and thankfully, she did. I hooked her collar to the lead attached to the railing on the front step. "This is for your safety," I told her. "And mine. I don't want to have to chase a coyote." More prescient words have never been spoken.

My coffee in hand, I sat with Breezy on the front steps. She stared at the woods on our right, up the small hill. She was squeaking and vocalizing. I knew something was there watching us, but I wasn't able to see or hear it. A deer? Raccoon? This went on with Breezy squeaking for ten or fifteen minutes until I decided I needed a coffee refill. I had barely gone inside and started pouring coffee into my mug when Breezy barked excitedly. I went from 0-60 mph in moments, tearing around the corner in the kitchen and flew down the front stairs. "Outta my way!" I yelled to one of the cats. She's always directly underfoot when the action hits.

I burst out the front door. Breezy was on full alert, looking to her right. I looked there also. The young male coyote that had been hanging around was now slinking toward us, coming down the hill next to the house. It was a scary sight. The sneaky bastard had waited until I went in the house to refill my coffee before he made his move. One thing you can say about coyotes is that they are incredibly smart. He was on his way to attack Breezy on the steps, but he obviously had underestimated my reaction time, probably figuring me for a total lard ass, and that he would have plenty of time to get to Breezy before I came back outside. Well, he'd be right...I *am* a total lard ass, but I can move like the wind when I need to.

I yelled at him with my usual colorful vocabulary, and he darted toward the back of the house. Breezy was barking the whole time at full volume. Against my better judgment, I ran in the opposite direction around the other side of the house, looking for a weapon as I ran. The only thing I saw was a plastic fence post. I supposed I could jab out his eye with the metal spike on the bottom, so I grabbed it on my way past.

*There he was!* He stood in the backyard by the garden pond, bold as day, practically posing for me. "Get outta here! Go!" I yelled. He ran into the woods. I then foolhardily turned my back on him and walked away, yelling at him the whole way. Dumb move, but I didn't think he'd come after me.

Several years passed, and the coyotes, which again had been fairly absent, began returning in droves. It does seem to be a two-year cycle and for some odd reason they do this every time right before I start writing my next book. Somehow those suckers know. I guess they want to be sure they get to be in a few chapters.

My fifty-year-old wooden baseball bat had been dusted off and now went with me whenever I went outside. I hadn't felt the need to carry it for protection for quite a while. The other night, a coyote was howling like mad somewhere in the pasture. I went out the back door and yelled, "Hey! Shut up!" I had forgotten that Rambo (that's what I call the guy who bow hunts in my back pasture) was still in his tree stand out in the back forty. He texted me from his perch and said, "Wow. That coyote means business." And yes, he had heard me yell at it; unfortunately, sound carries very well in the quiet of late fall. Good thing I didn't swear at it like I normally do—that would have been even more embarrassing.

Breezy knows that the coyotes stalk her. Rambo said he thinks that's what all the howling is about—they're trying to lure her into the woods. For once she was actually sticking close to me rather than running after them like she had done for years.

# Chapter 12

# Misbehaving Minis

Either Misty or Sunny is the one being naughty when the mini horses get their hooves trimmed—and usually, it's Misty. This particular time, Kate the farrier had successfully trimmed three of Misty's hooves, but on the last one, Misty kept kicking. Kate has the patience of Job and is incredibly calm, but eventually, she had enough and told me to go get Sunny while she dealt with Misty. Kate has been a farrier for years, plus she has regular-sized horses of her own. She doesn't put up with any crap, especially from mini horses.

Kate tied Misty's lead rope to the outside of the corral panel on a short lead so Misty couldn't hurt herself, but she wasn't able to move much at all. Having never seen Kate angry, I concluded that she must have been really pissed. Misty was in full lockdown mode and wasn't happy about it, but she couldn't do a damn thing about it.

I went to get Sunny and led her out to Kate, and she began to trim her hooves. Having nothing else to do while I held onto Sunny's lead while she was being trimmed, I looked over to see that Donald, the goat, was inside the corral trying to bust Misty loose

Misty wearing a crocodile head for Halloween.
Proof that I don't just do this stuff to Donald.

by pulling on the knot with his teeth. Misty was looking at Donald with a forlorn look, pleading, *Get me outta here!* She pawed at the ground with her front hoof and heaved a heavy sigh. She knew she was trapped.

I laughed at Donald as he worked diligently to untie the knot and free his buddy. If Kate had tied the knot differently, I think he would have succeeded. He was really working at it. It's a good thing she knows how to tie a knot that a mini and a goat can't untie.

Kate's been trimming the minis' hooves for years. At one point, she looked up from trimming Sunny. "You used to have a llama, didn't you?"

"Yup," I replied. We both thought about it for a while, neither one of us much missing the llama. "Remember me chasing Misty and Sunny all over the pasture trying to get a halter and lead rope on them so you could trim them?" I asked.

"Yup. It's much easier now," Kate replied. That was the understatement of the century. It's easier because the minis are no longer out in the three-acre pasture. Instead they live in a detached two-car garage with an enclosed outdoor pen. Even with this smaller area they give me a work out when I try to corner them. They can work up a good head of steam running fast in circles past me.

I looked up to see Kate's four-year-old daughter over by the garden pool. She was looking at the water lilies and the weird stuff I had floating in the water. Like a toy great white shark that rears its head above the water and puts the fear of God into the masses of frogs that have made that little pond their home. I swore I heard the little girl say, "Super pretty!"

I turned to Kate. "Did she just say 'super pretty'?"

She glanced over at her and snorted. "Probably."

I told her about the great white shark and, having bared my soul that much, I proceeded to tell her about the toy dinosaurs rampaging through my hosta garden. She paused in trimming Sunny's hoof and looked up at me as I continued, "Yeah, I go to garage sales and fight the little boys for the dinosaurs." I realized how weird that made me sound and said, "Yeah, I'm weird." That nearly got a full-fledged laugh out of her.

T-Rex on a rampage in the hosta garden.

Her daughter trotted over, and I told her about the dinosaurs. At least she didn't think I was wacko—probably because she was only four. She ran to find them and came back with a handful. I let her pick out one to take home. She chose a T-rex. Good choice, kid. My first college major was Geology—I wanted to be a paleontologist and dig up dinosaurs. I eventually switched to an English major, but I still love dinosaurs.

Donald gave up on trying to bust Misty loose and went to find something to eat. Misty hung her head in resignation, knowing that she still had to let Kate trim that last hoof. Just another fun-filled day on the hobby farm.

## Chapter 13

# Circle of Life

On this particular morning, after I went outside with the dog, I noticed the crows were noisier than usual. Several of them perched in trees on the periphery of the yard, cawing their little black hearts out. I decided it meant one of three things: 1) *There's a hawk, let's get him!* 2) *There's an owl, let's get him!* or 3) *Our servant just put out grub, let's get some!*

After putting out a liberal portion of cracked corn and bread chunks in the usual spot, I settled onto the front step, a rug under me to keep me warm since the temperature was hovering in the low forties. The minis and Donald were fed. Nutter the cat was on his leash under the bird feeder, eating grass. Breezy was next to me on the steps. It would have been a peaceful, Zen type of morning—the sky a clear watery blue, the sun cresting over the woods—had it not been for the abrasive *Caw! Caw! Caw!*

The infernal racket moved to the big oak tree near the minis' garage. Two crows erupted into the air, chasing a smaller bird. Was it an osprey? Some type of small hawk? They harried it, nipping at its tail as they flew next to it. The hawk veered and swooped toward us. I was up from the steps in an instant, standing over Nutter and waving my arms as I craned my head back to look up. "He's not for you, buddy! Find something else to hunt!" I yelled. The hawk circled above Nutter and me until the crows dive-bombed and drove it away. "Thanks, crows!" I crowed, though I knew they didn't do it for us.

Again, the commotion—hawk and crows erupted upward from another tree. The chase was on. The hawk disappeared behind the house. I grabbed Nutter and retreated to the steps to sit with the dog. Breezy's head was on a swivel, on alert, looking for the predator. She could tell from my tone of voice that something was wrong, even if she had no clue what I had said. "You need to look up, you two! Not only at the woods," I nagged at both cat and dog.

The hawk suddenly shot over our heads; a surprise strafing run from behind the house. A big crow launched upward from the oak and plotted an intercept course on the fly, meeting the hawk directly over our heads and drove it off toward one of the ponds.

Nutter and Breezy on the steps.

This went on for at least ten minutes while I protectively held Nutter's leash. He knew something scary was afoot and hadn't moved a muscle. The hawk swooped in circles above us, eyeing Nutter. It eventually landed in the birch tree next to the bird feeder and watched us from fifteen feet away. The crows continued to harry it until it got tired of being harassed and went to bug someone else.

Fast forward to a few months later, to a beautiful, warm September dusk.

Breezy was out in the front yard doing her business and I was sitting on the steps watching and guarding her, ready to attack anything that went after her. A bright red male cardinal was on the bird feeder having a snack before bed. I heard

Owl feathers I found on the road.

the other birds making alarm cheeps in the trees around the yard. I knew something was going on and looked toward the minis' garage in time to see a large bird swoop to land in an oak tree on the edge of the woods and immediately blend in.

The cardinal was still perched on the feeder, oblivious to the threat. I told him to be careful. Two more cardinals flew to the birch tree next to the feeder. "There's an owl over there. Keep your eyes peeled," I told the newcomers.

Sudden movement to my right: The owl was making a beeline toward the feeder. I jumped to my feet and lurched toward the feeder. "Watch out!" I yelled. "Go, guys, go! The owl is coming!"

The birds scattered to various tree limbs as the owl glided silently past. I've never seen one in flight that close—it was maybe ten feet from me. It had been coming straight at us, only twelve feet above the ground. It flew between the feeder and the tree with the birds and glided to the pasture. I walked over to the birch tree and looked up at the cardinals, "Are you guys okay? Holy crap, that was close, wasn't it? I was almost as scared as you."

I shouldn't be surprised that the predators all come close to my house. The bird feeders are a hotbed of activity, and that has to look mighty tempting to a hungry owl or raptor and, of course, the coyotes. I've never seen a great horned owl here although I've heard them in the woods, but I have seen numerous barred owls and, one night, barn owls. They have pale faces that stand out in the gloom and have an incredibly eerie, ghostly call that makes the hair stand up on the back of your neck.

Twice now, I've witnessed small hawks after they've snatched a bird from either a feeder or the ground. Once, it was a blue jay; the other time, it was a cardinal. I'm not sure what kind of hawks these are—they are smaller than red-tailed hawks, but just as deadly.

The day the hawk grabbed the blue jay, I was in the house when I heard a loud thump and wings hitting the front window. Then I heard a struggle and panicked chirping out on the front patio. I thought a bird had hurt itself from hitting the window and went outside to check on it and see if I could render aid.

A small hawk was on the patio with a blue jay between its talons. The hawk wasn't much bigger than its prey. The blue jay struggled to get free while the hawk dug in with its talons and beat its wings to cover the jay so it couldn't escape.

I stood on the steps five feet from this life-and-death struggle and tried to talk it out of eating the blue jay. "Hey, you. How about you let that poor thing go? There has to be something else for you to eat around here. I know—I have some canned cat food. Maybe you want that instead of that poor little blue jay?" No one could ever accuse me of having a good grip on reality. Who else would think to have a conversation like that with a predator? Me, that's who.

Its eyes were fierce and piercing as it glared up at me. Like with the owl, I'd never been that close to a hawk, either. It was beautiful and scary, all at the same time. I was glad I wasn't a bird. It would suck to have to watch your back all the time with things like that always gunning for you. I continued to try to talk sense into it. Yeah, right—it's not like I was even remotely talking sense.

The hawk had listened long enough. He gathered up his wings, tightened his grip on his prey, and launched into the air with the blue jay clutched beneath him. I lost sight of them as he flew across the pond. When you think about it, it's kind of gross that a bird would eat another bird. It's like being a cannibal, in my opinion.

The cardinal was far luckier than the blue jay. That particular day, I noticed the small hawk on the birch tree, a cardinal clutched tightly in its talons beneath its chest. I pounded my fist on the window, startling it enough that it lost its grip on the bird, which immediately flew to hide in a juniper tree. Probably thinking, *Well, you can't win them all,* the hawk remained in the tree and eyed up the remaining birds at the feeder, ready to make another selection. I darted out the front door and told it to get the hell out of there—the birds were off limits. It flew away, and I walked down to the juniper to check on the cardinal. He was understandably jumpy and chirped with terror. "It's okay, I got rid of it," I said. "I'm glad I could save you, but I'm not going to be around all the time. You need to be more careful."

It was a mid-January day with a beautiful, delicate blue sky and a bright, cheery sun. And oh, did I mention it was fifteen-below-zero and, factoring in the wind, it was a delightful thirty-below wind chill? It was colder than snot outside.

I knew the birds would need extra sustenance because of the cold, so I put corn and pieces of bread out in the snow like usual. To the normal fare, I added unsalted peanuts in the shell for the blue jays, crows, and squirrels, plus an added bonus for the crows: a soup bone with lots of meat on it—I had gotten it on clearance at the grocery store. The night before, I'd also rolled peanut butter into balls, which I'd placed in the freezer to make frozen treats for the squirrels. The critters wouldn't go hungry.

An hour later, I was sitting at my kitchen table when I noticed a big bird perched on a nearby dead oak limb. A crow? I wondered. No, it was too big, plus it had a white tail. I saw two much smaller crows busily dive-bombing it, cawing madly. The large bird turned its head and from its profile I realized it was a bald eagle, holding something in its talons and eating it. The crows continued to harry it, and it dropped whatever it was holding, which fell thirty feet below into the freshly fallen fourteen inches of fluffy snow. The eagle flew down and began hopping up and down in the snow, searching with its talons for what it had dropped. Had he caught a squirrel? A bunny? A bird? It was fascinating to watch and I wanted to see how it all played out.

The crows continued angrily swooping at the eagle, who was still on the ground. I watched transfixed through the window, motionless, but still, it somehow saw me. It stared straight at me and we locked eyes for a minute or two. It's not often you get stared down by an eagle. It gathered itself up and took wing with its prize tucked in its talons.

That's when I realized what it was—the crow's soup bone. As the eagle flew away with it to the pasture, I laughed with delight. He had stolen it right out from under the crows. And were they ever pissed! I wished I had seen him soar down the driveway and swoop down to snatch up the soup bone. That would have been awesome to watch.

Another day, when I went out to feed all the critters first thing in the morning, the turkey flock was waiting for me like usual, but this time, they didn't come running when they saw the ice cream bucket full of corn. They weren't behaving like they normally did, and all of them were making a noise I had never heard them make before. I looked around the yards, and woods to see if there was a coyote or maybe another turkey flock but didn't see anything that would cause them to act that way.

I poured out the usual little piles of corn so each of them would have something to eat and they still didn't come running. Something was definitely up and, me being me, I had to find out what it was. I walked slowly toward the turkeys and said, "What's wrong with all of you? You're acting weird. I've never seen you not come running when I put the corn out." Their heads were swiveling around, and they were still making that odd noise. I scanned the yard again but saw nothing that would alarm them until I decided to look up and saw a huge bald eagle perched in a tree nearby. Yeah—I'm pretty sure that would make a flock of turkeys nervous. It made *me* nervous. I walked toward it and it launched itself into the air and swooped away across the pond. The turkeys all heaved a huge sigh of relief (okay, I'm imagining that, but I'm sure it happened) and high-tailed it over to the corn.

Not long afterward, I was driving down the road on my way somewhere. At least twenty crows had landed on the side of the road and more were perched in the trees to each side. All were loudly cawing back and forth. A group of crows is called a "murder" of crows. I prefer the more technical term, and that's why I call them a "shitload" of crows.

I drove my car closer and slowed down to see what the excitement was all about. The crows flew up and scattered into the surrounding trees, cawing loudly. I rolled down my window, glanced down into the ditch on my left, and saw the rib cage of some unfortunate deceased animal. I'm not certain if it had been a deer or a coyote, but it was big. The crows had been happily tearing chunks of meat off it and weren't too happy that I had inserted myself into their mealtime.

Noticing the sudden silence, I looked up to see the massed crows perched in the bare trees, their beady eyes appraising me. I felt like

I was in a Hitchcock movie, and the scary music was about to start. I'm talking about *The Birds,* and I was Tippy Hedren. I quickly closed my window and peeled the heck out of there before they could dive-bomb my car, shatter the windshield, and peck me to death.

Since we're on the subject of predators and prey, did you know that mink are able to climb trees? One rainy day, I had come out of the chicken coop and saw Breezy near the back edge of the yard. She had been sneaking off lately as she had done every spring, and I began walking over there to nab her before she disappeared. I saw what I thought was a huge black squirrel coming down the side of the big oak tree. It saw me and climbed back up the tree. Then it came back down. I wondered if it was a groundhog since it was so large, but I didn't think they could climb trees like that.

I walked closer—I know, dumb move, but when have I ever not done dumb things—and I realized it was a huge, honking mink. It ran back up the tree, and then I saw what it had been hunting—my favorite mallard duck couple. They were swimming in the back garden pond. I walked over to the pond until I was about five feet from them and pointed at the nearby oak tree, "Ummm…you might want to get out of there and go somewhere else because a mink is right there in that tree, and it looks like it's hunting you." I grabbed Breezy and went back in the house. The ducks must have listened because I saw them the next morning, still alive, when I put out the corn for the breakfast buffet.

I had no idea mink could climb trees. Breezy never saw the mink, although I could tell she smelled it. I told Rambo about it, and he warned me not to get anywhere near it because they're mean, not to mention they have sharp teeth. Too late—I had walked right past it when I went to warn the ducks. I've gone up against coyotes; I'm not going to let a mink scare me.

## Chapter 14

# Tossed Aside

I will never understand why people think it's okay to dump their unwanted items on the side of the road. Since the road I live on is sparsely populated, a car or pickup truck can easily pull over, and stuff can be tossed with no one witnessing it.

Today, it was a Christmas tree. They didn't bother to at least toss it into a ditch so it wasn't visible and could molder away near the other plants and bushes. No, they tossed it on the side of the road, in plain view. Have these people never heard of putting it in their household trash? Or perhaps not getting a damn tree in the first place if they can't figure out where to dispose of it.

All manner of things is dumped—mattresses, tires, yard disposal bags full of leaves—you name it, it's been tossed somewhere on our road. What really pisses me off is when they throw things into the ponds.

I assume most of this nefarious activity goes on in the dead of night, but I have sometimes seen cars pulled over on the side of the road in the middle of the day and people acting suspiciously with their trunk open or tailgate down. That's when I pull my car up like I'm stopping to say hi, and take a peek to see if there's trash in the back of their car or truck. If I see any, I turn my attention back to them and then stare at their license plate. They get the message and quickly hop in their car and leave.

One cold winter afternoon, I was heading home after work. In the distance, I saw something lying on the side of the road and wondered what new trash had been dumped since I'd last passed by. Pulling up next to it, I saw it was a medium-sized kennel. The front door was off and lying on the road a few feet from the kennel. I thought that was a little weird. Why would someone dump an empty kennel? I parked and went over to investigate. Inside the kennel were a towel and some pet food, and I realized some complete dickhead had dumped their pet and left it on the most isolated stretch of the road. The animal more than likely freaked out when cars drove past, broke out of the kennel, and ran for the woods.

I looked behind me across the road from where I was standing. It was a cattail-filled swamp and I doubted the animal had headed over there. On the side nearest the kennel were woods and, past that, a pasture. To get there, it had to climb down a steep bank, jump across a five-foot wide snow-covered creek with running water in the center, and run up another steep bank. I shaded my eyes with my hand and tried to look for tracks in the snow leading over to the woods. Not having any luck with that I decided to whistle, figuring it was a dog and that might call it to me. I whistled a few times and then said, "Here, puppy! It's okay." Pausing to listen, instead of a dog, I heard a loud, panicked meow. From further into the woods, another cat meowed. I could tell they were terrified.

The poor cats had been dumped on the road and left there to fend for themselves in the middle of winter! It was maybe twenty degrees that day. Did the people who did this really think someone would come along and take the cats home? As if leaving them in a kennel with a towel and some food absolved all their responsibilities to their family pets. I was livid.

I knew I couldn't leave them there—it would be far too cold overnight, not to mention the coyotes are thick in that area; plus, what would they eat? The cats would never survive. I stood there trying to figure out how I could catch them, knowing they were freaking out and wouldn't come to me, particularly since they were cats. I also tried to figure out how the hell I would make it down the steep bank, across the creek, and climb the far bank to get to them. I talked to them and told them to hang on, I'd be right back. One cat was hiding in a section of metal culvert; the other was somewhere in the woods.

Jumping in my car, I peeled away for home. Once there, I grabbed two small kennels and placed inside each a can of cat food and a bag of cat treats. I also changed into my shit-kicker boots that I wore when I worked in a cargo facility. Those suckers have a deep tread that is perfect for snow and ice-covered terrain. If I was going to leap the chasm, I needed the right footwear.

I drove back to the kennel and parked my car. Grabbing my two kennels, I called to the cats to make sure they were still there. Okay, I meowed. What else would you expect from me? The one in the culvert answered me. A kennel in each hand, I looked down the bank to the creek. Holy crap, how was I going to accomplish this? I can barely walk in a straight line, and I was planning on traversing terrain that was more suited for a mountain goat.

Before committing myself to it, I looked both ways down the road to make sure no cars were coming so no one would witness me flailing down the hill, or see the huge splash when I ended up on my ass in the creek. I knew I couldn't make it down holding both kennels, so I lobbed first one kennel and then the other across to the far bank. Thankfully, they didn't roll into the creek.

This photo was taken from the road. You can't really see how steep the two sides are. The creek is at the bottom of the photo, and the culvert is crosswise in the woods in the top middle.

The snowmelt had filled the creek to its banks, and the ice-cold water was cruising along merrily. I wasn't looking forward to possibly falling into it.

Spying several small bushes and trees, I grabbed at them as I slid down the bank and hung on tight to one when I hit the bottom. Thankfully, the one I was hanging onto didn't break. Next, I eyed the creek. How the heck was I going to leap that damn thing? Maybe when I was twenty and moved like a gazelle, but I was now in my late fifties, and I was nowhere near as graceful.

*Whatever,* I thought. *The cats need me to help them. If I fall in, I fall in.* Unfortunately, I didn't have enough room to back up and take a running start, so I just went for it. Sailing through the air, I landed on the other side and immediately grabbed onto another bush to stop from falling backward into the water. Holy crap—I'd done it! Now all I had to do was climb the steep bank, wrestle two cats into kennels, and then turn around and make it back to my car, this time while holding two kennels. How I get myself into these pickles, I have no idea.

I was now technically trespassing on someone else's land, but I figured they would understand. Only one car passed by, and they didn't stop. They probably wondered what the hell I was doing up there with two empty kennels and meowing loudly to something no one could see. Thank God I can't see what I look like when I do things like this. I'd have to go into witness protection.

The cat in the culvert watched as I slowly approached, and it darted backward deeper into the culvert. I set down the kennels, opened the door of one, grabbed a can of cat food and cracked the lid. "Here, kitty, I have some nummies! Come on out, and you can have some." I knelt down in the freezing cold snow and held out the can so it could smell it. The cat meowed several times and slowly crept forward as I held the can close to the end of the culvert. I have no idea when the poor thing had last eaten, but it was obviously starving because it emerged fully from the culvert and chowed down. It let me pet it, and then I picked it up and it allowed me to place it into the kennel without a fuss. I was surprised because its last kennel experience hadn't gone so well for it. Maybe it knew I was trying to help it.

One cat down, one to go. I meowed for the other cat and heard it meow back. It sounded like it was further away than it had been. I called and called for it, but couldn't see it and eventually, the meows stopped. I had no idea where it was or how to catch it. I looked down at the cat and said, "Can you tell your buddy to come over here? He needs to come now because it's going to get dark soon, and he can't stay out here. It's not safe." It was too busy scarfing up the cat food and ignored me. I wasn't ever able to catch the other cat, and I feel awful about it.

Heaving a heavy sigh, I grabbed the empty kennel and then picked up the one with the cat, and holy crap, that thing weighed a ton. Lurching over to the edge of the hill, I looked down. Well, I could toss the empty kennel over to the far side, but I'd have to carry the one with the cat. This time, I slid on my butt all the way in the snow to the bottom. I couldn't grab at the bushes fast enough while I was so unbalanced with a heavy kennel in one hand, so I gave up and slid. My boots got a little wet in the creek, but I didn't slide all the way into the deep part. Now, I had to leap across. I got up, brushed the snow off my pants, and lifted the kennel. "Hang on, kitty! This is gonna be a rough ride," I said as I leaped across. God knows how I did it, but I somehow made it. Then, it was onward to drag myself up the steep bank while holding the kennel. I swear that thing weighed twenty pounds, and I was out of breath by the time I made it up to the road and my car.

I grabbed the kennel the dickheads had left and placed it in my trunk to get rid of on the next trash day. At least one person knows how to dispose of things properly. The kennel with the cat went on the front seat next to me, and, while the car warmed up, I tried to figure out what to do with him now that I had rescued him. It was a male with grey fur, and he seemed like a really nice cat. He purred when I reached into the kennel and scratched his chin. He was a sweetie, and I couldn't figure out why someone would want to get rid of him. Years ago, I would have adopted him, but I had enough cats and dogs at home and didn't need to add any more. Then I remembered that the feed store in town fosters cats for adoption. That's where I'd take him. They'd know what to do with him.

Once we arrived, I left the kennel in the car, went into the store, and told them the whole story. Turns out they foster cats for a local animal rescue organization but they couldn't take him from me—I needed to bring the cat to the animal rescue. Back in the car, I called the number they had given me and explained that I had a cat someone had dumped on the side of the road. "God, I hate when people do that to animals!" the person at the animal rescue said. "Bring him down to the veterinary clinic that we use. They'll check him out and then we'll find a foster family for him."

I drove to the nearby town and brought him into the clinic. In the short time I'd known him, he'd really grown on me. He would have been a great cat, but I stayed strong and didn't keep him. I said goodbye to him with tears in my eyes, praying that his next family was a good one and he lived a long and happy life.

For the next few weeks, every time I drove past the section of road he had been dumped, I looked for the other cat. And yes, I meowed, hoping it would hear me and come, but I never saw or heard it again. I hoped that it had made its way to one of the neighbors and they had taken it in, but I'll never know for sure.

## Chapter 15

# A Deer Friend

I was mindlessly engaged in my normal morning ritual of putting out cracked corn for the various critters who visit me each day. As I poured a small pile of corn here and there on the driveway near my front garden pond, my peripheral vision caught movement of the big and brown variety, a color I normally associate with "coyote." The caveman part of my brain screamed *Predator! Bad! Run! Run Faster!* I gave an involuntary gasp as my head jerked up to identify whatever was approaching while my hand flew to my chest in fear. Meanwhile, my prefrontal cortex had finally gotten off its lazy ass and chastised the caveman part, *No, that's not a coyote, dumbass, that's a deer. Not "predator." Not "bad." Settle down, okay?*

I can't blame myself for nearly freaking out—the deer was only about ten feet away, edging toward the corn and me. I don't think any of the deer have come that close to me. It may have been one of the yearlings that had visited with their mom the past year. Their mom had always been friendly, and so her two youngsters were as well.

My favorite deer licking her lips for the bird seed.
Try to ignore the overgrown "lawn."

The corn was all poured out and I stepped back a few paces and stood as still as a statue and waited to see if the deer would come any closer. And she did, taking tentative steps forward until she was so close that, had I leaned forward and stretched out my arm, I could have touched her. I was in shock that she trusted me so much. I continued to stand quietly, and for once, I didn't blab on and on about nothing.

She was absolutely beautiful with large brown eyes and long eyelashes. Periodically, she would raise her muzzle from the corn and look into my eyes, then go back to eating. Her feet ended in tiny black cloven hooves, and she stamped them lightly onto the ground a few times. It was fascinating and awe-inspiring.

The minis and Donald were behind me in their pen, clamoring for hay, so I said to my new friend, "Okay, I'm going to back up now, so don't get scared." She looked up at me and watched as

I backed away. Any other deer would have headed for the hills long before then.

She came back a number of times and visited after that. One afternoon Breezy was stretched out in the hole she'd dug under the hammock, and I was sitting on the back patio nearby. A deer emerged from the woods and approached us from the other side of the black walnut tree. I wasn't sure if it was her, but when she came within ten feet of Breezy, I was certain. She and Breezy gazed into each other's eyes and I couldn't believe Breezy didn't get up to chase her. The deer turned to look at me before wandering to the front yard. That moment was incredible.

I absolutely loved that deer—she was so sweet. One day, Breezy, Misty, and I were in the park, walking the trails. Misty loves being in the woods. Suddenly, a deer appeared in front of us on the trail and stood there, watching us. Misty is used to the deer being around and she wasn't concerned. She was having too much fun. The expression on the deer's face was like, *What are you doing here? I've never seen you over here!* I knew it was my favorite deer, so I stopped and talked to her. Breezy also seemed to recognize her and didn't bark at all. Normally, she chases deer and barks like a maniac.

After a time, the deer moved away further up the trail and then turned back to wait for us to follow her. She did this several more times before going into the thick underbrush and, once again, she turned as if she wanted us to follow her. If I hadn't been with my dog and mini horse and had been wearing jeans instead of shorts, I might have gone into the brush to see what she wanted to show me. It was the oddest thing—I kept thinking of the fairy tales I used to read when I was a child where the wild animal does this. Or maybe I'm thinking of *Snow White*. I'm not really up on my Disney movies.

She disappeared into the deep woods, and Breezy, Misty, and I continued on the trail and headed home. Maybe she had given birth to a fawn and wanted to show me. I have no idea.

A month later, my friend Bridget came over bearing a bottle of wine, and we sat on the back patio, ate dinner, drank wine, and talked. She said, "Look! There's a deer over there," and pointed to the woods. The deer emerged and watched us.

I jumped up, "That's her! My favorite deer!" and I walked toward her and talked to her. She tentatively came closer, but she had never seen Bridget before and was hesitant. "I'll go get you some yummies," I said and went to get some corn. She was waiting for me when I came back. I poured some onto the grass and backed away while she ate. Bridget and my wine glass were waiting, so I went back and sat down, and we watched the deer eat her treat.

It doesn't take a lot to make me happy—and watching deer makes me happy.

## Chapter 16

# Your Wish is My Command

The crows have me trained. It was barely light outside in the middle of winter and I was staggering around the kitchen with my first cup of coffee. I heard them calling outside. I tried to ignore it, but I couldn't. It's hard to miss the strident calls demanding, *Where the hell is the corn? Give us the corn!*

By the time I was coherent, dressed, and went outside into the frigid nine-degree morning, they had gone. I brought their food outside knowing they'd be back. I looked up to the sky, and far off in the distance, I could hear them. The corn was out, and the pieces of bread were tossed amongst the corn kernels, but no crows. It looked like I would have to call them in. I gathered the air deep into my lungs, put my shoulders back to open my chest, extended my neck, face up to the sky and let 'er rip: "*CAW! CAW! CAW!*"

Really anemic and rather embarrassing, even to me. I do a much better turkey call—and you should hear me quack like a duck. I also do an excellent impression of a coyote; however, I do it to run the bastards off. The crows and ducks hear me calling in their language and come running—I mean flying.

My faux crow call reverberated throughout the countryside and echoed back to me. *Crap. That really went a long way*, I thought. How embarrassing if anyone knew it was me making that noise and not a crow. I can imagine the neighbors thinking, *That wasn't a crow! Who is that nut case?*

Moments later, an answering *Caw Caw Caw* came from about a quarter mile away. I answered back and, from the north, in swooped a crow, and it did a fly-over to check out the grub I'd laid out. The crows know it's me when I do my daily crow call. They probably think I'm a nut case, too, but they answer me and come swooping in soon after they hear my pathetic attempt at mimicking them. I do a really crappy crow imitation. Can you picture me standing alone, except for my dog, in my driveway first thing in the morning, making various birdcalls? No one else around, just me and the dog, and I'm loudly doing one bird call after another. If there's one motto for my life, it would be this: *Thank God no one can see me when I do crap like this!* Except sometimes they can. Once again, it's no wonder I'm still single.

After cawing loudly like a crow a few times, I happened to look out to the road and noticed one of the park maintenance trucks parked there. Good God. Did they see me toss my head back and utter full-throated caws? Worse, did they *hear* it? I scuttled back into the house, grabbed my coffee, and snuck to the window, trying to stay out of sight of the road and hoping to see a descending horde of crows.

I am one of the few people who like crows. Actually, I love them and always have since I was young. I tend to align myself with the underdog. *Someone* needs to like them. At my previous house in a suburb, my elderly neighbor, Jim, fed the neighborhood crows and thought I was trying to steal them away from him when I put a bird feeder in the backyard by our shared fence. His crows never came to my feeder, however. They chose instead to dive-bomb me and try to peck my head. Crows are selective about their relationships and are loyal to a fault—and they were fiercely loyal to Jim.

When I moved to this house, I tried to make friends with these country crows, but they had always ignored me and my pathetic attempts to gain their favor and trust. That is until the infamous April blizzard when I first began putting out corn for them. It changed my relationship with the other animals as well—the ducks, turkeys, and deer. They began to trust me because they knew I was trying to help them.

Finally, the crows had begun visiting daily to gobble up the piles of cracked corn. I was so excited about it that I brought out stale bread too. One cold, snowy winter day, I found raw hamburger in the fridge that was going bad. I was about to throw it out, but then I remembered how much crows like to eat dead animals and figured the hamburger would be the same thing to them. I left the whole pound of hamburger out next to the corn and retreated into the house to watch. Crows descended *en masse* and devoured it. Another morning soon after, it was fifteen degrees outside. Breezy and I put out the corn in several piles, and I added roast beef that was going bad. Maybe I should eat my food once in a while. I went back into the house to pour another cup of coffee and heard the crows calling. I looked out to see sixteen…then eighteen…and finally twenty crows, all gobbling corn; the beef long gone. I went to grab my camera and snuck up to the window, but they'd already taken wing and flown above the house. I may have heard a grudging "Thank you" as they shot past.

Huge, fluffy snowflakes drifted down in a swirling dance driven by the wind. It was so peaceful watching the snow coming down. Once again, silence reigned supreme; the usual spring cacophony of bird song had been muted. They were in survival mode now—forget about courtship and mating.

Another middle-of-April snowstorm had begun, and I thought back to the previous year's storm and how brutal it had been as I filled the bird feeders. I went outside several times that day to refill them and was greeted each time by an endless stream of chickadees, juncos, nuthatches, cardinals, blue jays, woodpeckers, and squirrels. Everybody was clamoring for food.

In mid-afternoon, Breezy decided it was time to go outside again. I suited up in my winter parka and filled the ice cream bucket with corn, and we went out into the snowstorm. Mr. and Mrs. Mallard Duck were walking up from the pond. If I were a duck, I'd have flown rather than trundled through the snow. When Mrs. Duck saw me, she made an arrow toward me. I put out the grub and she barely waited for me to back away before she dove in.

Later, the geese and wood ducks showed up and were digging in the snow, trying to uncover the corn. The geese walked across the yard toward the pond with the snow already up to their bellies. A lone mallard drake passed them on his way to the food. He bulldozed through the snow with his much shorter legs. He had to have been exhausted by the time he made it all the way from the pond.

I went to feed the minis and Donald, and then walked up the driveway to take photos of the snow falling over the ponds. It was beautiful. On my way back to the house, I took the time to shovel away the snow to make it easier for everyone to find the food. The corn supply was dwindling, so I substituted chicken chow. It has corn in it, so I thought they might eat it. I was wrong. Mr. and Mrs. Duck were again slogging through the snow toward me. I pointed to the chicken chow, "Your food is right there," and went inside the minis' garage to refill their water buckets, then I went in their outdoor pen to take photos of the ducks eating. The hen noticed me and came over to me, then walked along the outside of the pen past me and along the side of the garage.

I stepped out of the garage, and Mrs. Duck came right up to me, cocked her head, looked at me, and muttered quietly. Her hubby stayed back. She looked meaningfully at the bucket of chicken chow and then back at me. I laughed, "Okay, fine! I'll get you the good stuff!" I went to the house to get the remaining corn. When I returned, she waited patiently as I poured some onto the snow. She allowed me to get within five feet of her. I was shocked. I backed away, and she dove in. Her husband had retreated to the yard. He wasn't so sure of me.

Mrs. Duck in the snow.

Summer arrived, and I'd made more friends. My favorite mallard drake that returns every year was now allowing me to sit down on the driveway, three feet from him, as he ate. I don't think I've ever been that close to a wild duck. He completely trusted me. I sat in companionable silence with him as he gobbled his lunch. Wood ducks are shyer and flightier compared to mallards. If wood ducks see a person, they tend not to stick around. It got to the point that, while I was putting out the corn, I would look up to see several wood ducks perched nearby on a tree limb (this type of duck nests in trees) watching me. They would wait for me to go in to the house before swooping down to eat. Eventually, they trusted me enough that I could stay outside and sit on my brick flower planter to watch them as they ate.

The geese also warmed up to me. I've heard about geese attacking people, but these had never tried. I watch their body language and adjust my behavior accordingly. Sometimes, that means I back away slowly, talking softly to them. The same goes for the turkeys. It's only the coyotes that I run straight toward to chase them away. You'd think I would be smart enough not to do something like that, but I've done it so many times I've lost count.

One morning, the mallard duck couple watched me bring out the corn. They wandered up to the front steps, and the drake was at the storm door, looking in at my cat, Nutter, who was looking out at him. They were nose-to-bill. The duck stared at the cat, and Nutter stared back. They were inches away from each other, only the glass separating them. The duck wasn't scared, and Nutter wasn't interested in going after it. It was a moment of inter-species harmony. I wish I had a picture of that; it was incredible to see.

The next day, the ducks walked up from the front pond when they could easily have flown instead. The turkeys had eaten all the corn, so the ducks wandered to the backyard garden pond and swam for a while. I noticed the drake at the back door, standing there, staring into the porch. Maybe he was getting ideas about being a house duck. You never know around here. I walked out to the porch and asked him, "Want some bread?" He wasn't afraid and waited for me to go back inside to grab the bread. I snapped a few photos of him through the door and then I opened it. He and his wife moved a few feet away while I tossed the bread pieces toward them. Later that day, I saw him nuzzling the back of my SUV. His wife was watching him, looking exasperated, and she turned and went to the front garden pond to swim, leaving him there. He continued to admire his reflection, and rubbed his bill on the bumper. He turned to leave and must have noticed the movement of his reflection so he went back to nuzzle it some more. A narcissistic duck—who'd have thought?

Mr. Duck waits patiently at the back door
for me to bring him a treat.

Soon enough, a bald eagle flew above as I sat on the front steps, and then a hawk flushed three drakes from the corn pile; they flew off squawking. Turkey after turkey trotted down the driveway to eat. Breezy sat next to me on the steps, nonchalantly watching it all.

Four hawks flew with strident calls from tree to tree nearby. The songbirds abandoned the feeders and ducked and hid in the bushes near the front patio. I told them, "One good thing about having me sitting out here is that I can scare them away for you." I stood up and waved my arms at the hawks and they skedaddled. A lone female duck was swimming in the back garden pond. I'm not sure where her hubby was.

I never know what I'll see when I open the door in the morning to let Breezy out. One day, it was a crow eating corn, while nearby, the male mallard duck was again admiring his reflection in the mirror-like back bumper of my black SUV. He caught me watching him primp and flew off embarrassed, returning later to

Why did the turkey fly on top of the car? Because it could.

chow down on corn. Sometimes, I see a turkey with a crust of bread in its beak, running around the yard and being chased by the rest of the flock who all want his bread—even though more bread is right in front of them. The strangest thing I've witnessed is a wood duck and a raccoon, only a few feet from each other, sharing the corn.

Early on an April morning with a distinct chill in the air, I put out the daily breakfast buffet of cracked corn. A crow winged in, perched in the oak tree, and observed. I heard a duck quacking repeatedly nearby and knew it had to be the one I call the "crazy hen." I have noticed her for several years running because she does not shut up. When she's flying, she quacks nonstop. When she's swimming in the big ponds, she quacks nonstop. She's loony, but whenever I hear her, I laugh because it's too damn funny. It sounded like she was somewhere in the backyard, so I decided to sneak up the hill around the house and discover why she was being more vocal than usual.

As I came up the rise along the side of the house, I was sure I'd see her by the back garden pond, but couldn't spot her anywhere. The *quack, quack, quacking* was still going on nonstop. Where was the incessant quacking coming from? I backed up about ten paces from the house and gazed up toward the roof and suddenly, a duck's head popped up over the edge and looked down at me.

*She was standing on top of the roof.* I've never seen a mallard duck do anything so weird. The wood ducks will perch on branches and nest in trees—but a mallard? They are strictly land and water but never a roof. Bemused, I asked her, "What the heck are you doing up there?" She stared down at me with a look that fairly dripped with scorn. *What do you think I'm doing? I'm on your roof, and I'm quacking, you fool.* With one last, lingering look of disdain, she took wing and flew to one of the ponds, quacking maniacally all the way.

That's when I realized where she'd been—directly above my bedroom. She had been trying to get my butt up and out of bed so I'd go out and put down some grub. She may be crazy, but she's not dumb!

Another morning, I noticed two turkeys with eight fluffy little babies in the backyard. They saw me looking at them from the bay window and darted toward the woods. Nutter was lying in his cat bed watching them and I said, "I wish I had my camera right now." Soon, I forgot about them and sat down at the table. Ten minutes later, I looked up to see one of the hens, five feet from the window, staring in at me. Then, the second hen did the same. It made me laugh. They were nice enough to come back to give me the perfect photo op, but I still didn't have my camera, so they posed for nothing. Their babies were somewhere out in the yard. I hadn't mowed for a couple weeks, so I could barely see them in the long grass.

Now the turkeys perch on my roof and look through my windows.

The late autumn sun hadn't begun its slow rise from behind the trees lining the back pond. It had been snowing like mad when I went to bed the night before and I had no idea what I would be waking up to outside. Rolling over in my warm covers, I heard the turkeys and crows making noise like usual, clamoring for me to come out and feed them. Clomping and gobbling sounds came from above me— it sounded like one or more turkeys were on the roof of the house. They'd begun flying up there and hanging out, I guess for the view, or maybe the crazy hen had told them to do it. The geese and ducks were now long gone, migrating on their way to their winter vacation getaway. When I finally got up from my warm bed and peeked out the bedroom curtains, I saw thirteen turkeys hanging out near the bird feeder, looking miserable and cold, and several crows perched in the oak trees. Braving the cold, I opened the window and called out, "I'll be right out. Hang on a few minutes!" The turkeys perked up when they saw me. Yes, I'd done this same thing before—pretty much every morning. That's how the crazy hen knew where my bedroom was.

Eventually, I stepped out the front door with the bucket of cracked corn for the turkeys and birdseed for the feeders and noticed Rambo's truck parked near the minis' garage. *He's nuts*, I thought. *Why would he want to slog through the snow-covered woods and climb thirty feet up to sit in a stinking tree to hunt before dawn?* Ugh. I could think of far more captivating pursuits, such as curling up with a good book or digging into chocolate cheesecake—or maybe both at the same time. Yes, I have no problems eating cheesecake in the morning…or anytime.

Turkeys crowded around me as I poured corn onto the ground. First, of course, I needed to clear away the snow with my boot so the corn didn't disappear into the snow. The turkeys dug in, and then I filled the bird feeders. I noticed a lone deer by the pine tree, near Rambo's truck. Gee, Rambo doesn't need to go to his happy place way out in the pasture—the critters come right up to his truck! The same thing happened last spring when he was way out in the back pasture hunting. I spotted the turkeys hanging out next to his car. I snapped a few blackmail photos to email to him, just to rub it in.

The turkeys don't let the deer get anywhere near the corn. I was surprised a

A couple of stud-muffin turkeys hurrying to get some corn.

turkey could chase away a full-grown deer, but they can, and they do. As the deer meandered closer, several tom turkeys looked up, and when it got too near their breakfast, they ran toward it, flew a few feet into the air, and did a quick twist and turn to try to slash it with their spurs. When this happens, the deer will invariably turn and run. I find it so fascinating that a much larger animal can be intimidated by a bird. I wanted to tell the deer, "Stand your ground and fight back! You deserve corn, too!" It could easily take on the turkeys and run *them* off and claim the bounty of corn for itself. But it chooses not to, instead running away in fear. Why is that? And why does that remind me of how some people act?

Later that morning, I was replenishing the corn near the bird feeder. The turkeys saw me and came running toward me from the pasture and stood a few feet away, cooing and purring in turkey talk. I poured out small mounds of corn here and there so everyone would have their own pile as I talked to the turkeys. I don't remember what I said; actually, I don't remember most of what I say, anyway. As I blabbed on and on to my turkey buddies, I glanced up to see Rambo

Nutter keeps an eye on the turkeys.

with his bow in hand by his truck, standing stock still and looking at me in bemusement. The mass of turkeys was now less than two feet from me, gobbling up their feast and trusting me completely. And not far away was the apex predator, also known as Rambo, a stone-cold killer of just such creatures as these, watching me hanging out with the turkeys. I could tell he was amused. He actually has a huge heart and isn't one of those guys who hunts only because he wants to whack things. It seems to me that being out in nature and being a part of it is the most important thing to him.

A few days later, I woke up to this: October 20 and an eight-inch snowfall that made it into the record books for that date. Ugh. Turkeys were once again waiting at the feeder. After I fed them and the birds, I blazed a path in the snow to the chicken coop carrying the ice cream bucket of chicken chow. I was nearly there when I had a weird feeling. I stopped and looked back over my shoulder to see fourteen turkeys in single file on the path, following me to the coop. I cracked up laughing, but it did remind me of that scene in *Jurassic Park* with all the velociraptors swarming around. They're cute and funny…until they tear your throat out. When I opened the coop door, the chickens saw the huge turkeys and ran to hide.

I drove to town to go to a store, and the cashier, in a plaintive tone, asked, "Why is it snowing so early?" I looked at him and said, deadpan, "Global warming." He didn't think that was too funny.

Sundown comes early in late October. I hurried home from work one night and was greeted by the turkeys waiting impatiently for me as my car came down the driveway. That night, they slept in the oak trees near my bedroom. They had never roosted near the house before. I guess they wanted to be close to the breakfast buffet. Smart move. In the morning, when I emerged with the corn, they spied me from their perches high in the trees and, one by one, glided down with wings spread to land past me with a thump in the yard. Turkeys aren't the most elegant birds when they fly. They are huge, though, so when one flies right past your head, you notice it.

True joy is when you're outside in a blinding snowstorm, squatting down under the bird feeder, holding a bucket of cracked corn, with a flock of turkeys circling around, and one brave little one trusts you enough to come within two feet of you, to eat the corn you've thrown down.

I was out there for at least ten minutes like that. It was magical.

They actually stuck around watching Rambo yesterday. But they skedaddled when he headed in their direction. They know an alpha predator when they see one.

I've been putting out corn for two years now, and, even when the weather makes me think twice about going outside, I think I'll keep doing it because I love watching whoever decides to show up for the buffet.

Oh—and remember how I've joked about people being able to see me when I'm doing weird stuff? I was on a walk with Misty one day and stopped to talk to a woman who lives a few miles away but walks down my road a lot. At one point in our conversation she said, "I see you outside feeding the turkeys all the time." I tried to keep a completely blank look on my face while inside a small voice was screaming, *They really can see me! Gaahhh!!*

## Chapter 17

# Speckles Flies the Coop

On one of the last nice days before the blustery cold and snow of winter crashed down upon us, I sat in a lawn chair in the chicken run while the chickens ran around nearby. At that point, Violet and Sable were still in control of their shared brood of nine chicks who could now be considered teenagers. The chicken run isn't remotely secured against predators—I'd worked on fixing it the previous spring but lost my ambition and said the hell with it. Instead, I would need to be present to protect the chickens whenever they were outside. Fair enough. I settled down in my chair with a book and soaked up the warm autumn sun. Everyone was having fun either chasing insects or snatching up tender, green delights from the ground. Normally, there's bird netting draped above the chicken run that I take down before the snow comes, since the weight of the snow causes the netting to end up on the ground where I invariably trip over it. Since the netting wasn't in place, I needed to keep a keener eye for any airborne predators, and I periodically glanced upward and scanned the sky for incoming.

The younger chickens were still hesitant about being outside under the open sky; they'd step out of the coop door and bravely place one foot on the ground, testing the waters, so to speak. One of their siblings would push them from behind, and they'd screech in terror and run back into the coop to hide. Eventually, they all crept out for a few moments, and a couple of them bravely joined Violet and Sable near my chair. Feeling that everything was going well, I turned my attention back to my book. Of course, that's when all hell broke loose.

Someone in the coop decided to freak out for no particular reason, and several chickens exploded in flight out the door. I managed to corral all of them except for Speckles, a tiny Japanese bantam, who flew over the chicken wire on the closest side of the run. It's the side that is closest to the woods and the steep hill down to one of the ponds. She landed about ten feet away and looked around uncertainly. The chicken wire was between her and me, with no easy way to retrieve her.

"Come on, Speckles…you don't want to be out there all alone. Come on back over here so you're safe," I pleaded.

She darted into the brush for points unknown. I hurried to put the rest of the chickens back into the coop. "Sorry, guys, but the fun's over. I have to go rescue her," I said as they grumbled about being locked up again.

Once everyone was safely tucked into the coop, I walked out into the yard and over to where I thought she might have gone. "Speckles! Where are you?" *There she was!* I saw her peeking up at me from under a wild raspberry bush. I slowly approached and talked softly to her. It was her first time completely alone, and she had to be terrified—except she wasn't. She was having the time of her life. Rather than come to me, she turned tail and took off down the hill toward the pond. I guess she was choosing freedom over safety. I wasn't going to follow her down that steep hill. I'd tumble head over heels the whole way down and end up at the bottom with at least two broken bones. But a tiny chicken would have no problem in that terrain.

I called for her for a while but gave up and went back to the coop to update the rest of the chickens. "I don't know if we'll ever see her again. She ran down the hill. I hope there's no coyotes around because she won't last very long." I think Violet and Sable as her co-parents may have been a tad worried, but the rest of the brood was tucking into their chicken chow and didn't look up. I went back to my house, deciding I would come back out to look for her a few more times before dark. If I didn't find her by then, she would more than likely be some lucky predator's meal by morning.

I had no luck the next two times I walked around the edges of the yard, calling for her. I even clucked like a chicken. No response. She was laying low. As dusk settled in, I went back outside to give it one last try. Once again, I called for her and peered under every bush. I heard her clucking and moving somewhere in the tall weeds so I called for her again, but she shut up and went silent, probably so I couldn't triangulate her position. Chickens are smart that way.

I went to the coop and got Violet, thinking I could lure Speckles with her. Carrying her close to my chest, I took her up to the pole barn, thinking it was where Speckles was hiding. I held Violet out in my hands and asked her to make a few chicken noises. She managed to cluck a few times, but her heart wasn't in it. Still no sight of Speckles, so I brought Violet back to the coop, set her down and thanked her for her effort.

As I said good night to all the other chickens and commiserated with them that they had probably lost a sister, I opened the door to step outside and saw Speckles near the coop. She was on the other side of the chicken wire, where she had first made her escape. I talked to her, but she still wouldn't come closer. I figured I was scaring her, so I sat inside the coop with the door open, hoping it would draw her in since the other chickens were getting ready for bed and making noise.

I had to stop one of the roosters several times from darting out the door. After twenty minutes of sitting there and no Speckles, I was sick of waiting and I went outside. If she wasn't there, screw it. I'd had enough of chicken chasing. She would be on her own. Then I saw that she was perched on the chicken wire, ready for bed. She probably thought it was a great place to sleep. She had no idea that she was a prime target for the owls that were hooting in the nearby woods.

She looked at me. I looked at her. She wouldn't come. Chickens can be stubborn. I knew if I tried to grab her, she'd freak out and fly away. I moved the lawn chair to face her and sat down to wait for full dark. Chickens can't see well in the dark, and I hoped if I waited long enough, I could grab her. She watched me, and I watched her. Her eyes got heavy, and she looked like she was about to fall asleep. After her big day of adventure, I could see why she was tired out. I swatted mosquitoes and watched the yard for coyotes and raccoons, getting more and more freaked out because I don't like being out after dusk anymore. That time of night had always been my favorite—until I met the local coyotes.

I'm not sure how I figured out how to do this without alarming her and causing her to fly away, but as it got darker, I slowly got up from my chair and crept toward her. She watched me but didn't move. I approached her from head-on and, with glacial slowness, I reached out both arms in front of me about two feet apart. I crept closer and closer, and with a pincer movement, I snapped my hands together and grabbed her like a tiny football. *I got her!!* She squawked loudly and flapped her wings, trying to escape. I held on tight and made it into the coop, where I put her on the roost between her buddies. She complained the whole time but settled in to sleep.

The owls would have gotten her for sure that night if not the raccoons or coyotes. She had absolutely no idea—and yet she was mad that I ruined her fun!

# Chapter 18

# Manure Madness

There I was, engaged in my favorite activity in the world—shoveling manure. You do realize I'm kidding, right? I tend to put it off for as long as I possibly can, but I was back at it again. Scoop, lift, fling. All too soon, the wheelbarrow was full, which meant after unloading it, I'd need to fill it again. And again, and again.

Misty and Sunny were out in their outdoor pen eating hay. Donald, meanwhile, had been "helping" me load the wheelbarrow. His definition of helping is to get in the middle of whatever I'm trying to do and make it ten times more difficult to accomplish. As the manure rose in the wheelbarrow, he sidled over and tried to tip it over with his shoulder. I'm pretty sure he thinks he's funny. "No! Knock it off, Donald," I said. "I don't want to do any more work than I have to, and you are not helping. Go away and bother some-one else." He went to harass the minis for a while, but soon enough, he was back.

Somehow, I managed to keep it all from tipping over as I pushed the manure-filled wheelbarrow toward the door. I had to outsmart

Donald because I knew he'd try to get out once he saw me open the small garage door as I wheeled the whole mess out to dispose of it in the woods. I positioned the wheelbarrow so that the door could barely open, grabbed the wheelbarrow handles, pushed it outside, and swiftly slammed the door shut. Donald pushed against the door from inside with his head, but it was too late. I'd won. That time, anyway. I filled and emptied that wheelbarrow so many times I lost count. And each time, as I pushed it out the door, a major struggle ensued between me and Donald, who wanted to escape and go have some fun.

Have you ever tried wrestling a 195-pound goat that is all muscle? I have, many times, and I'm not even close to all muscle anymore, although I'm still fairly strong. He refuses to give up, but so do I. Guess that makes me as stubborn as a goat. Lately, he had been acting like a jerk to Misty; he seemed to consider her lowest on the totem pole behind Sunny and then him. I saw him mounting Misty (as in trying to have sex, no matter that he was gelded or that she is a horse and he is a goat) as a means to show her who was boss. Animals are like people—if they sense the slightest whiff of weakness, they go for the jugular or, in this case, the posterior.

Several times, I witnessed him barrel straight at her, head down, and T-bone her in the side of her belly with his head. It had to hurt. Goats have hard heads; the males fight each other for dominance by charging at each other and smashing their heads together. Worried that he was hurting her, I yelled at him, but he did it a couple more times. I bopped him on the nose with my fingers to try to get him to stop, but that didn't do a thing. Poor Misty. I said to her, "Why don't you kick him, Misty? You could kick his ass. He thinks he's better than you. He's not."

After I'd seen him head butt her in the side a few days in a row, I decided to step in. I chased him around inside the garage until I caught him. I wrapped my arms around his long neck to hold him and snaked my right arm under his belly behind his right front leg, locked my hands together at his chest, then applied a full nelson and hung on tight. He bucked and reared, but I wasn't about to let go. I put my face next to his and hissed, "You aren't going anywhere until you quit hurting Misty. I'm not putting up with this crap, Donald." I hung onto him for at least five minutes, and it took all my strength. I was so mad that I could have body-slammed him to the ground, but I didn't want to hurt him. "You do know, Donald, that

Donald, pretending to be innocent.
(photo courtesy Annette Herman)

you don't have to live here. You can go up to Dan's house to live with his goats. Do you want that, Donald? I'll call him right now, and you can move out of here. I'm not letting you hurt Misty ever again." He settled down eventually, and I let him go.

I thought about that day as I was struggling to get the manure-filled wheelbarrow out the door. After all the shoveling and transporting manure, I decided I was too tired to care if he muscled past me, and the next time he shoved against me trying to get out, I let him.

"Go ahead, Donald. Try not to get into anything. And stay close so the coyotes don't get you." I didn't have to worry since he does tend to stay nearby and comes running when I call his name. He's more like a dog than a goat. He trotted a short distance away to investigate something as I trundled the wheelbarrow out to the woods with the newest load. Suddenly, Donald was prancing straight at me, his head down. *Boom!* He hit the wheelbarrow head- on, which was exactly what he intended to do. I'm not sure how, but I kept the whole pile of manure from tipping over and continued onward. Here he came again. *Boom!* A few piles of manure fell to the ground. It was kind of funny, but then again, it wasn't.

I'd manage to go a few feet, and he'd circle around and come at the wheelbarrow again. It was like I was the matador, the wheelbarrow was my red cape, and Donald was the charging bull. I was laughing at first but then I became annoyed. "Stop it! Why are you doing this? *Arrgghhhh!!*"

This same thing happened every time I removed the manure. I decided the next time that I would outsmart him, so I grabbed an armful of hay and tossed it in the outdoor pen. The minis and Donald trotted right over and dug in. I pulled shut the big garage door so Donald couldn't get inside the garage and bother me while I was slinging and shoveling but I forgot how devious he could be. He stood on his hind legs and peered in through the windows from outside but realized he couldn't get in that way. Unfortunately, the big door doesn't lock and can be opened by hand…or head. I heard the door rolling up and then slamming back down. I turned around, holding the shovel, and glanced at the door, watching it rise, then slam shut. He was pushing hard against the heavy garage door, lifting it with his head. I snorted and said, "Good try, Donald. Sorry, buddy, but you can't get in."

I went back to shoveling. After a while, you kind of go into a Zen state. Scoop, lift, dump. Scoop, lift, dump. Plus, it's good exercise. I was spacing out, deep into my manure reverie when I felt something pushing against my butt. It was Donald's head. He looked up at me, his eyes shining with triumph. *You think that was impressive? Just wait until I achieve world domination,* I imagined he was saying. He had managed to lift the door high enough that, before it slammed down, he was able to dart underneath. He must have timed it perfectly. That is a smart goat. Smarter than me because I didn't think he could do it. In the future, I knew I'd have to wedge a short length of 2 x 4 wood along the upper rails so he wouldn't be able to lift it more than a few inches.

I sighed and kept shoveling. Sometimes, you have to go with the flow. Or the manure.

## Chapter 19

# Playing Possum

Mid-January in the depths of winter. And I discovered I had an opossum living in my garage. It took me a while to figure it out—things were knocked from shelves and broken, and I swore I hadn't done it. I thought it might be mice, but the items were too heavy for a mouse to move.

Trash day arrived, and I went to grab the garbage bag I'd left inside the garage a few days before and haul it up to the trash cans at the end of the driveway. I couldn't figure out why all the garbage was strewn around *outside* the bag and scattered all over the floor, but for some reason the garbage bag still looked full. I squatted down to pick up the various bits of debris, meaning to put it all back inside the bag, which I now absently noticed, had several large, ragged holes torn in it. What the heck? I scratched my head but didn't think too much about it, not until I tried to pick up the garbage bag—which seemed rather heavy for not having any garbage in it—*and it moved.*

I screamed and ran. "*Breezy! Breezy! Help! What's in here? Sniff it!*" Breezy is always up for excitement, and she ran over and intently sniffed the bag with gusto as it continued to move. Deciding it probably wasn't a great idea to have her nose next to some type of unknown and possibly fierce critter, I grabbed her collar and put her in the house before whatever was inside got out and attacked her. Grabbing a rake, I poked at the bag, and a tuft of grey fur popped out of one of the holes. Some type of critter was definitely in there. I wasn't sure if it was a raccoon or what, but I wasn't up to the task of removing it.

I ran inside the house, grabbed my phone, returned to the garage, stood about ten feet away watching the bag move, and called my brother in a panic. "Omigod…there's something in my garbage bag. *Arrgghhhh!* It moved again!" I screeched. "*Omigod. Omigod.* What do I do? Can you come help me?"

He couldn't be bothered. "I don't want to get bit," he flat-out refused. "Drag it outside. Or call the cops." As he listened to me hyperventilate, he repeated, "Just pull the bag out of the garage." Right. I was *so* going to do that. Why the hell did he think I called him if I was going to try to handle it on my own? I guess he thought it was okay if I got bit. He hung up, and I heaved a huge, long-suffering sigh and returned my gaze to the moving garbage bag. What in God's name was I going to do?

I grabbed a shovel and tried to get it under the bag, thinking I could carry the whole thing out into the yard. The bag moved more violently. More grey fur stuck out through one of the holes. What kind of animal was in there? Was it going to leap out at any second and rip me to pieces? I screamed some more and ran. Picking my addled brain, with what few brain cells I still have, I tried to think of someone, anyone, who would be willing to help me remove the bag and whatever was in it from my garage.

I hoped it would find its own way outside and left it alone for a while. I went back after about an hour, but the grey fur was still there. Sigh. I picked up the phone and, swallowing what little pride I had left after all these years of hobby farm mayhem, I once again ended up calling the local police to assist me. I swear they must have a full dossier on me by now and an entire file cabinet devoted to me, with all the times I've called them to help me out of another pickle—mini horse escapes, rabid woodchuck roundup, someone shooting arrows into my front lawn from a quarter mile away, the neighbor's horses stampeding around my yard at three in the morning.

The cops know *exactly* who I am, unfortunately. I'm sure I've provided plenty of entertaining fodder for their morning donut and coffee breaks. I can imagine them cackling, "Did you hear what she called us for *this* time?" a cop would say as he slurped his coffee. "No, *really?* You have *got* to be kidding me!" his buddy would reply as he wiped powdered sugar from his mouth. In the first few years I lived here, I had relied on my long-suffering neighbor, John, who I kept on speed dial. He helped dig me out of numerous unfortunate situations in the past. Realizing that he didn't need to have a nervous breakdown along with me, I instead turned to the local constabulary, and the rest is history.

When the dispatcher answered my call, I explained the situation, saying it was *not* an emergency, although it certainly was one for me. Eventually, a squad car made the trek down my long driveway and pulled up next to the mini horses' garage. Out stepped a guy who was barely out of high school. He seemed too wet behind the ears to actually be a full-fledged police officer; I don't think his whiskers had even grown in yet. He hitched up his uniform pants and moseyed over to see what the fuss was about.

He turned out to be what is euphemistically termed a "community service officer." A baby cop. *They sent me a baby cop.* I guess I can't blame them. *Real* crime needs to be addressed by *real* cops. Mysteriously moving garbage bags? Well, that would be the perfect scenario to test the gumption of a cop-in-training.

Unfortunately, he wasn't up to the task. I had high hopes when he first stepped out of his squad since he looked like a farm boy. Alas, I was wrong. He had absolutely no farm sense or animal knowledge whatsoever, and I had to do most of the work. I had to tell him exactly what to do and when to do it. It's not like I knew what the heck I was doing since I'd never been in this particular situation before, but at least I am able to improvise when needed. And I'm able to think like an animal if I have to. He just stood there like a lump. He didn't even have a gun! I know because, after scanning my eyes over his uniform, I asked where his gun was.

"No, they won't let me carry one yet."

"Then what the hell are we going to use to kill this damn thing?!" I sputtered.

He shrugged. I gritted my teeth and turned to grab the shovel and poked repeatedly at the garbage bag. The grey fur suddenly erupted out of one of the holes, and that's when I saw the intruder was an opossum. I guess that was better than it being a raccoon because those suckers can be nasty.

Both of us jumped back, worried it was about to attack, but the opossum, now free of the garbage bag, instead scuttled a few feet and hid under a wood pallet. I poked underneath the pallet with a rake handle. The opossum hissed and curled up into a tight ball. Baby cop pushed the pallet with his shoe since he obviously didn't know what else to do. The opossum darted out and hid under something else. I was worried it was going to disappear underneath my sports car that hadn't run for years, and if it did go under it, we'd never catch the damn thing.

Baby cop didn't have a clue. I had to hand him a snow shovel and tell him to guard the back of the car to keep the opossum from running underneath. I would have been better off doing the whole thing myself but since he was there, I tried to get him to understand how to think like an opossum. It was hopeless.

I got smart and opened the other garage door closest to where it was hiding. Both of us then poked at it together, and it ran out the open door and headed for the hills.

It took us an entire hour to wrangle the opossum out of the garage. I had to tell the kid what to do every step of the way. He was not happy at all. The critter...not the cop. The cop was beyond clueless.

The opossum hissed and snarled at us and his pointy, needle-sharp white teeth were prominently displayed when I

A thoroughly depressed opossum after being evicted.

took his photo after we chased him out of the garage. He was fifteen pounds if he was an ounce—a big 'un. Baby cop hiked up his uniform pants, keyed on his microphone, and called in to headquarters to say in cop-speak that he was clearing the premises. I couldn't wait for him to leave.

I could tell the opossum was sad it got kicked out of the nice, warm garage. It came back a number of times after that, looking for birdseed and hoping to regain entry to the toasty, warm garage. Breezy noticed, ran over, and barked at it. The opossum promptly curled up in a ball next to the house, playing possum. I went to look at it, and it was so scared its teeth were chattering. It wasn't cold outside that day, so it was fear, not hypothermia. I told Breezy to leave it alone, and I apologized to it for the dog scaring it. Poor thing. It was kind of cute. Except for the long, pink rat tail—and the needle-sharp teeth.

## Chapter 20

# Night of the Living Snappers

The two cats were on leashes as I sat with them on the front patio. It was nearly dusk on a warm September evening, and Breezy was running loose somewhere in the yard while I was happily sitting on the patio chair enjoying the weather. Nutter pounced on something in the flowerbed, and Breezy ran over to help. I figured it was a frog or maybe a toad. Nutter was playing with whatever it was. "Is that a toad? Don't eat the toad, Nutter. I think they're poisonous," I said.

I went over to look at what he had found,

A baby snapping turtle. They aren't this cute when they grow up.

and no, it wasn't a toad. It was a tiny, dirt-covered, newborn snapping turtle. I went inside the house and grabbed a plastic container and put the turtle in it, planning to bring it down to the pond.

Nutter was peering intently at a small hole in the dirt. I got down on my hands and knees to look and saw that something was emerging. It was a really creepy moment—like a campy 1950s horror movie. Another baby turtle was clawing its way free from the hole. I realized a mama snapping turtle had laid her eggs in my flowerbed, only feet away from my house.

Like I said, it was like a horror movie where the zombies wrest themselves free of their graves and emerge dirt-covered and ravenously hungry. I was fascinated and repelled all at the same time; I'd never seen turtles being born before. As I peered down into the hole, I watched as the turtles struggled free of their eggshells under the ground. They had to be exhausted from doing that, but they then had to climb the steep dirt walls, which crumbled under their sharp little claws. A herculean task for anyone, and these turtles had been born only a few minutes prior. It would be like a newborn human baby having to climb a monumental cliff using only its bare hands. And we humans complain if we can't get a parking spot right by the store and have to walk a few extra feet. We don't have it so bad. We just think we do.

Nutter and I watched, fascinated, as more and more baby turtles emerged. I don't know how they did it. The hole was maybe a few inches in diameter, with steep sides. The turtles dug into the dirt with the claws on their tiny front legs and heaved their little bodies upward. They rested and then resumed climbing. Other turtles were moving up from below, jockeying for position and sometimes pulling each other back down.

I helped a few make it out, then went back inside the house for another container since the first one was getting full. I soon had two plastic containers filled with milling, muddy, baby snapping turtles.

I counted twenty tiny turtles and more were still in the ground. I finally put the cats inside because they wanted to eat them.

A blue jay perched directly above me on the bird feeder and talked to me, probably wanting me to let them loose in the grass so it could gobble them. My lawn was totally overgrown like usual and it would have been a struggle for the little turtles to power through it all the way down to the pond.

Breezy helped me bring the twenty turtles I had collected down to the pond. I plucked them out of the containers one by one and placed them in the mud at the water's edge. Some rested, others plunged right in and motored off. "Have a good life!" I said and waved good-bye to the little buggers.

Back at the house, *more* were coming out of the hole. I shook my head and went inside to make dinner. An hour later, they were still emerging. Some were making their way through the lawn, struggling toward the pond, and some lay exhausted near the hole they had emerged from. I transported two more to the pond and then left the rest to fend for themselves. How many eggs did mama snapper lay? I saw at least thirty turtles. I wondered how many had made their way on their own toward the pond when I wasn't there and how many did the blue jays carry off?

The next morning the hole had been widened, and leftover eggshell fragments were strewn about, probably eaten by a raccoon. Luckily, it hadn't found them before they were

The first batch of mud-covered turtles in the container.

born—I've seen that happen often enough. I'll watch a turtle spend all day digging a hole and laying their eggs, only to see the next day that all of the eggs have already been dug up and eaten. These little guys were lucky.

## Chapter 21

# Duck Duck Grey Duck

Three days before the end of March and the ice was nearly off all of the ponds. The geese had returned nearly a month prior from wherever they overwinter, and the ducks weren't far behind—I'd never seen the geese come back during February before. It seemed far too early. My small garden ponds were ice-free as well, and that morning, I noticed the mallard duck couple taking their inaugural swim in one, while two deer browsed on the emerging plants nearby. Meanwhile, a lone turkey was busy at the bird feeders, stretching his beak upward to peck at the bottom of a feeder and gobble up the bounty of sunflower seeds tumbling out and onto the ground. The geese wandered up to see if the corn feed had been served, and a few wood ducks joined them.

As I gazed outside at all of them, I was struck by how they were all getting along. Ducks, deer, turkeys, geese—all co-existing in peace. We humans could definitely learn something from the critters at my house.

Sixty degrees brought the first hammock event of the season—and still in March! Breezy and I spent hours that afternoon soaking up the sun and snoozing. Life was good.

Spring had come early that year, and the winter had been mild and tolerable. The prior year was the winter from hell, to say the least. Oh, it started out fine; not much snow, temperatures hovering in the twenties. Once February hit, all bets were off. The other shoe had been dropped. Massive blizzards, subzero cold—I'm talking twenty-five degrees below zero. And it wouldn't quit; the snow was piling up into mid-April.

I don't normally mind winter; I'm not one of those people who says in early October, when two or three snowflakes drift down from the sky, "*Oh my God*, I want it to be *over* already!" A true Minnesotan would never say anything like that. Rather, it would be something like, "Bring it on! Yeah, I'm talking sub-zero temps and raging blizzards. Now, that's a *real* winter!" Not that I engage in many winter activities like a good Minnesotan should. I have never gone skiing, being far too uncoordinated, and the last time I drove a snowmobile was in the late 1970s when I crashed it into a tree and totaled it. (My brother had purchased it the day before. I'm not sure how I lived through that particular incident. Not the snowmobile crash—the telling my brother I had smashed up his brand-new sled.) I haven't skated in years, too afraid of how much it would hurt to fall on my butt on the hard, unyielding ice. Once in a while, I take the dog for a walk. Mostly, though, I spend the winter inside, reading yet another book and every so often looking out at the snow falling gently from the heavens, the wind whipping it into a blizzard, and the snow banks growing to ungodly proportions. That's the point where I get my lazy butt up off the recliner and go over to shut the curtains and block my view of the carnage outside.

It's funny that, with three large ponds and another small wetland on my property, the ducks come to swim in my small garden ponds.

The front one is an eight-foot round pond, while the one in the backyard is rectangular but not large or deep. The ducks swimming around in my little garden ponds rather than the nearby five-acre ponds is like the difference between me swimming in the ocean, or splashing around in a bathtub.

Late in the afternoon one day in May, I noticed a lone female duck out by the minis' pen looking for some corn to eat. The morning corn piles had been decimated already, and I poured some cracked corn into a container, then put on my winter parka before heading outside. (It was forty-five degrees. *In May.* Not exactly shorts and tank top weather!)

I walked slowly toward her. She backed away, watching my every move. I angled the container to show her the corn. "See...I have some yummies. I'm going to put them over there." And she let me do it. I was barely ten feet from her. She waddled toward me as the succulent corn showered down onto the driveway. I backed away and stood by the minis' garage and watched as the duck gobbled it up.

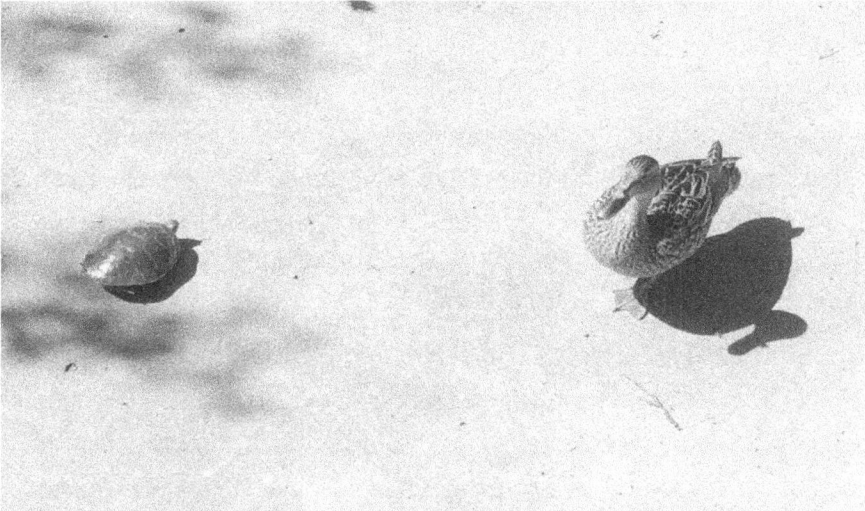

The friendly mallard hen came up to the house
to see what treats I might have for her. Not sure
what the painted turtle was doing there.

After eating her fill, she walked right past me and headed up the hill to circle around the house to swim in the back garden pond.

I went inside the minis' garage and up to the corral panels and squatted down to see how it looks to the minis and Donald when the ducks, turkeys, deer, and crows eat nearby. Misty stood by me, and together, we looked out. Donald pushed up to my back and snuffled my hair. He decided to rub his horn nubs all over me, marking me as "his," I presume. I told him he was weird and totally not my type.

Summer arrived, and early one evening, Nutter was on his leash, sitting in front of the house on the grass, hanging out with me. He never gets to go out unsupervised because of all the various predators. The minis and Donald were munching hay in their corral. Breezy barked and ran off to chase a turkey. A while later, she barked again, but this time, she ran to the edge of the woods where she has in the past scuffled with coyotes. *Bark, Bark!* Nutter was scared, so I scooped him up, put him in the house, and went to check on Breezy, who was still alerting at the edge of the woods. For once, she hadn't gone into full attack mode and disappeared chasing after whatever was there.

As I approached, I heard rustling in the brush. "Yup, Breezy, I hear it. What is it? A coyote? Maybe a raccoon?" I was feeling brave since I'd just finished an ice-cold beer. I peered between the bushes, and Mr. Duck looked out at me. What the heck was he doing in the woods, at the top of the steepest hill leading down to the pond? How did he get up there from the pond? I hadn't seen him waddling around the yard. I saw his wife a few feet back in the deeper brush.

He knew that I saw him, and I knew that he wasn't a coyote. All was good. I led Breezy away so she wouldn't bother them. Mr. Duck and his wife toddled out to go down and have their corn dinner. I walked to the driveway to sit in the chair I keep next to the minis' corral, near the cracked corn buffet and the ducks. As I sat there with my second beer, I nattered on about life to the nearby ducks.

Mrs. Duck ignored me and concentrated on the feast. Mr. Duck gave me a quizzical look but kept eating.

A few days later, the same friendly duck couple allowed me to slowly walk within fifteen feet from them as they waited patiently on the driveway for the corn to magically appear. I put some corn down and edged past them to sit on the rocks surrounding my front garden pond and actually pull some weeds. If I was pulling weeds, hell definitely had frozen over.

The drake turned to watch me, wondering what I was up to since I never go near "their" swimming hole. He later had his back to me as he ate, which showed how much he trusted me.

Breezy soon reappeared from chasing something in the woods and walked toward me. I warned her not to bother the ducks who were trapped between me and Breezy. She made a wide circle and eyed the ducks a few times, and with a big yawn and a whine—the dog version of stress relief—sat down next to me. I can't believe how

Mr. and Mrs. Mallard Duck in the front garden pond.

good she was with them. The ducks watched her but didn't move away. They trusted her. Wow. Breezy and I decided to walk out to the overgrown asparagus patch to see if any asparagus had managed to muscle its way through the weeds. None had, and I wasn't about to tackle that particular weedy mess. I'd already exhausted myself with the few weeds I'd already pulled. The ducks wandered over to the garden pond we had vacated and *Plop!* they hopped in to swim. It's funny to see them in such a small pond, but somehow, they manage to swim happily around, emerging to sit on one of the flat limestone rocks and preen themselves. Sometimes the drake sits on the rocks lining the pool and watches his wife swim. Then he falls asleep in the sun. It makes me smile. Watching the ducks fly overhead and then dive straight down to land in the middle of the tiny pond with a huge splash makes me laugh out loud.

Later that evening, it was time to put the minis and Donald to bed. I grabbed a bucket to fill their water containers. I walked to the front garden pond in my own little world, not paying any attention.

A sudden quacking and, with wings flapping, Mrs. Duck levitated straight upward from where she had been sitting on the edge of the pond and flew away. Mr. Duck stood there glaring at me. "I'm sorry!" I said, "I didn't know you were there. I couldn't see you." Yeah, because of how overgrown the damn thing is with weeds and sticker bushes.

He stood on one of the limestone rocks, and I couldn't get past him to go to my usual bucket dipping spot. I'm too lazy to walk all the way around the house to use the faucet there. I looked at Mr. Duck. "Okay, I can go over here," and I explained to him what I would be doing, step by step. "I need to fill this bucket for Donald and the minis, and I have to step up right here." I pointed to a spot not far from where he was. "I'm clumsy, let's see if I can manage it without falling in." He watched as I stumbled around on the edge of the garden pond, tripping on weeds. Somehow, I managed not to go headfirst into the pond. I stopped floundering for a moment and gazed at him, "You are such a handsome guy. I wish I had a camera right now." I was maybe four feet from him. I filled the bucket and hopped back down to the driveway, and told him to have a nice night.

Breezy and I were near the front garden pond a few days later. Donald was out with us, gobbling everything in sight. Now do you see why I have a goat? *They eat weeds.* That's a win-win situation. Two ducks walked up from the big pond and ate corn. Donald was being annoying, which he tends to be, and I put him back in the minis' garage while Breezy and I went to sit on the front steps while I ate my dinner outside. A female duck flew in low over the two other ducks that were eating. She arrowed back over them and shot between the house and the detached garage where the minis and Donald live. Suddenly, she blasted back over the roof above us. She must have executed a pinpoint 180-degree turn. She landed between the drake and hen and stood nonchalantly. She was more petite; the other hen was bulkier and quacked a lot. Which one was his mate? Was he stepping out on his wife with the crazy hen and had gotten caught?

The newcomer ignored him and calmly waddled over and started to eat. He watched her for a few moments and made up his mind. He lowered his head, his neck extended, and chased the first hen across the lawn. She protested but he ignored her and went over to the new hen and began eating. The first hen came back and forlornly quacked several times. He again chased her away, and she flew off, quacking nonstop.

He was being attentive to the second hen. I sat on the steps, fork halfway to my mouth. "Breezy, what in the heck is going on around here?" She looked over at me. "Was he two-timing the second duck?"

I yelled from the steps, "Hey, buddy! What's up with that? You're here with that other hen, and then, when your wife shows up, suddenly you act like it was all the first duck's fault that you were stepping out on your wife." The hen looked over at him as I berated him. I swear he had a sheepish look on his face.

Who knew ducks had love triangles and wandering husbands? Once again, I see parallels between humans and animals. We aren't that much different.

One afternoon, another duck couple was hanging out in the front yard. I'm not sure if it was the same pair. It's hard to tell by looking at them since they all look pretty much the same; I can only tell by their behavior when I approach them. Most of the ducks won't let me get close, but my favorite ducks have no problem with it.

A drake flew in from one of the ponds, and suddenly a knock-down, drag-out fight broke out with the first drake. Feathers were flying. Both of them flew away and went to continue the scuffle elsewhere. The hen hid in the grass. Lucky for her, I almost never mow, so she could duck down and blend into the long grass.

Eventually, four males dropped down from the sky and landed on the grass. The crazy hen walked up from the pond, quacking the entire way. They spotted her and started to stalk her, then they all went after her. Mallard ducks are brutal when it comes to mating, which is why I like the pair that swims in my garden ponds—he seems to be a real gentleman. He's always treated his wife with respect. Too bad the other males are a bunch of Neanderthals.

I walked over to three of the drakes that had hid behind the big spruce tree when they saw me approaching. "Don't treat her like that! What's wrong with you?" The crazy hen saw her chance and took off into the air. Two of them flew away also, chasing after each other and trying to catch her, back and forth, all of them quacking incessantly. I'm not sure what that was about—maybe their hormones were raging. They all came back and landed while the hen flew in circles around the area. I'm not sure if she wanted to be

Three of the reprobate mallard drakes.

caught or what. She comes back every year—I always know it's her because She. Does. Not. Shut. Up. The four males lined up on the driveway like fighter jets on an aircraft carrier deck and took turns flying after her. It was ridiculous.

I realized that the first hen was still hiding in the grass. She was no dummy. She didn't want any part of them. Finally, all the males flew off, but one came back, spotted her, and landed near her. It must not have been her hubby because she flew away in a panic.

Several years ago, a friend, Thomas, needed to find a home for his dog, Duke, because he couldn't keep him at his new apartment. I took Duke in, and he loved it here. Thomas would come out every few days to walk him and my dogs. After a while, he kiddingly accused me of "alienation of affection" because Duke liked me better than he liked Thomas. Eventually Duke passed away, but Thomas kept coming over to walk my dogs. He asked if he could bring over his roommate's pit bull, Iggy. I wasn't sure about it, considering what I'd heard about the breed, but it turned out Iggy was a complete marshmallow. And now he likes me better than he likes Thomas, too. I

Iggy. A total marshmallow.

mean, really—who can blame him?

On his way to my house, Thomas usually let Iggy run down the dirt road for exercise as he followed behind in his car. I don't really agree with doing that, but you can't tell Thomas anything. There isn't a ton of traffic on our road usually, so hopefully nothing bad ever happens.

On this particular day, as I looked out the front window toward the road, I noticed Thomas' car inching down the road and a dog racing along in front of it. Iggy would be coming down my driveway momentarily at full speed. The ducks were out there, eating corn, completely oblivious to the danger coming closer every second. I practically flew out the front door and nearly faceplanted down the cement steps. I stubbed my big toe, and it started bleeding. *Who cares, I have to save my ducks!* I thought. I ran toward the ducks while Iggy closed in on them from the opposite direction. I wondered who would get to them first. I waved my arms, "Fly, fly! *You need to FLY!*" They had never heard me yell at them like that and, uncertain, they stood and looked at me in confusion, still not clued into the lethal death force streaking at them from behind. Finally, they flew away.

I bent over, hands on my knees, huffing and puffing. I really do need to exercise more. Thomas pulled up in his car and looked at me like I was nuts. I glared up at him, "The ducks! *He almost got the ducks!*" It pissed me off. I turned and stalked back to the house.

The next time I saw the ducks, I gave them a talking to. I told them that Breezy was safe and would never hurt them. Iggy, on the other hand, might. They cocked their heads as I blabbed on and went right back to eating corn.

Iggy has now bonded with me enough (he does like me better, I told you) that he will stop in his tracks when I yell at him to leave the ducks alone. It might take longer to train Thomas to listen to me, however.

Whenever I put out the evening ration of corn, I always asked Mr. and Mrs. Duck that, if they had babies, could they bring them sometime so I could see them?

One morning, not long afterward, I looked out and saw Mr. and Mrs. Duck, with what looked like small birds eating corn next to her. That was unusual—the little birds normally keep away from the big ones. I grabbed my binoculars and gasped. She had brought her babies! I went out on the front step and Mr. Duck flew away. The hen watched me as I walked slowly down the steps toward them. She didn't let me get as close as she normally did—I was still far away when she toddled off with her five babies in tow, heading across the vast expanse of lawn toward the front pond. Okay, maybe I'm weird, but tears of joy were coursing down my cheeks as I waved at them, saying, "Thank you for bringing your babies!" None of the ducks had ever brought their ducklings before then, especially because traveling all the way from the front pond brings too big of a risk from predators. An eagle, hawk, or crow could swoop down at any moment and they would be…sitting ducks. Bad pun, I know. I stood there crying as they waddled away because it made me so happy that she somehow had understood what I had asked her to do.

The same ducks come back (the geese do, too, for that matter) every year. How do they find my ponds? What do they use? Maps?

GPS? I imagine the wife saying to her husband, *Uh, honey…I think you took a wrong turn back at Dubuque…maybe we should stop and ask for directions.* Yet somehow, they return, year after year.

# Chapter 22

# Chickening Out

I really thought I could do it and not be affected. I was so sure it wouldn't bother me at all. I couldn't have been more wrong.

My friend Bridget asked if I would be willing to raise chickens for her, which she would butcher and eat. "No problem," I told her when she asked if I thought I could handle it. "It'll be okay. I won't name them. As long as they don't have names, I won't care." I'm not sure what I was smoking that day because both she and I knew that wasn't true. She knows how much I love animals and that I've had chickens as pets for nearly fifteen years.

I ordered six chicks from the feed store and picked them up at the beginning of May. These were Cornish Cross chickens, bred to grow quickly and be in the grocery store by six to eight weeks. Just think of that—living for only two months. Some of my first chickens were this kind, and I feel sorry for that breed. They are basically mutants—they grow so fast they are in danger of not being able to walk, plus they were designed to have an excess of breast meat and thus are extremely top-heavy.

Once they arrived, I set them up in an area away from the other chickens and fed and watered them. Like I've had to do with other chicks, I had to pick them up and dip their beaks in the water because they didn't know what it was. Bridget asked that I only feed them organic chicken feed, and she paid for the 50-pound bags, which are double the price of regular feed. I also supplemented them with organic lettuce and apples because chicken chow gets boring after a while. Yes, I was already spoiling them, just like with my own chickens, but I stayed strong and didn't give them names. Like that was going to make a difference.

They got to go outside in a secure pen while Breezy and I whiled away the afternoons in the hammock. They loved sitting in the sun and feeling the breeze. I very much doubt many of this breed of chicken ever gets to do fun chicken things. The ones you buy in the grocery store are raised in huge buildings; all of them are massed together with no way to get outside and chase bugs or hang out in the sun. It's wrong, but I'm as guilty as anyone else—I buy chicken at the grocery store, too.

A month-and-a-half went by, and I was kind of hoping Bridget had forgotten about them. Even without names, I was getting attached to them.

One day, she called me to see how big they were. I walked over with the phone to look at them and said, "Oh, about the size at the grocery store."

A hen stopped eating, turned, and stared at me. "Oops. Sorry," I said to the chicken and walked away so they couldn't hear me talking to their real owner, Bridget.

The next day, I called Bridget when I was out with the chickens because the second fifty pound bag of organic chicken chow was almost gone. Those chickens ate like pigs. I snuck around the corner away from the chickens and whispered into the phone, "I don't want to talk too loud because they might hear me…Do you want them now, or let them get as big as turkeys?" She opted for turkey size.

*They knew.* They totally knew their days were numbered. I tried to stay strong when I was with them. I didn't want them to catch wind of what was in store for them, but they sensed it.

The day finally came—far too soon, and yes, for me it was

The chicks arrive home and are immediately greeted by a curious cat.

still unexpected. I was sure they would have more time to live, and that I would have more time with them. It's not like they had the greatest personalities or anything, although a couple of them were kind of sweet. I found out the night before that it was their last night on earth when Bridget called to say she would be over the next day. The next morning, somehow, they already knew. I went in their pen and squatted against the wall as they huddled depressed in the other corner. I cried and apologized to them. "If it were me, I would never do it," I told them. "I couldn't. Ever. I would let you grow up and have normal chicken lives. But you aren't my chickens."

They were freaking out. Eventually, they calmed as I petted their backs. One hen came and hunkered down next to me and looked up at me. I could swear she was pleading, *Save me!*

I went to see them three more times that morning before I had to leave the house for a meeting. I cried and cried. Snot was pouring out of my nose and dripping down onto the pine shavings. I was a complete and total mess, and so were they.

While I was at the meeting, I kept watching the clock and knew exactly when they were going to be whacked.

Once I got home, I ran to check their pen, hoping against hope that they were still there, waiting for me. The pen was empty. They were gone. Little white feathers were scattered here and there like they had put up a fight as they were carried to the waiting vehicle. I'm sure their little wings were flapping in terror. I sat down on the pine shavings in their empty pen and cried more.

I didn't ever want to know what they went through and told Bridget that she was never supposed to tell me. I couldn't handle knowing. I felt so bad for them but at least I know that they were spoiled rotten for the short time they were on this earth.

I could never do it. I could never raise an animal, build a relationship of trust with it, and then kill it. I can see hunting animals in the wild if you're starving and there's no way to get to the grocery store. But something you've looked in the eye and gotten to know? Never.

## Chapter 23

# Faster than a Speeding Mini

Over the years, the mini horses have made one escape after another. They seem to delight in outsmarting me. When they lived out in the pasture in an area enclosed by an electric fence, both Misty and Sunny would somehow manage to do the limbo underneath the bottom-most strand of wire. I don't know how they managed it with their fat bellies. Eventually, they moved to their current domicile, the two-car detached garage near the house. They have tons of room, plus I added an outdoor corral for them to enjoy the great outdoors. I used to let them out of their garage and supervised them as they munched away on the lawn. Most of the time, they were fine and stayed close by. Other times, they didn't and galloped off in one direction or another, with me chasing them and swearing the whole way. They seemed to think of it as a game. *Hey, I know…let's run off and make her chase us!* Misty would tell Sunny. *Then we can laugh at how stupid she looks when she runs while we make our getaway over to the neighbor's house.* And away they would gallop.

I had become an old hand at tracking them down, either on foot or by car, with the required bribe of the ice cream bucket full of grain, along with their halters and leads, once I somehow managed to catch them. I've gotten much better at catching them.

Misty is the smartest one—she never failed to figure out how to bypass whatever barrier or impediment to escape that I thought up. I put plastic fence posts along the entire side of the yard leading to the pasture so they couldn't escape that way, then attached bright orange snow fencing with zip ties the whole way. It looked like crap, but since no one can see my house from the road, it didn't matter. Then I realized they could instead run up the driveway and visit the neighbors that way. I went to close the massive metal gate my dad had installed back in the early 1970s. I figured the gate would effectively block off that means of escape since it covered the entire driveway, while the thick brush leading from the gateposts to the woods would take care of that part of the escape route. To make things even more diabolically difficult for the marauding minis, I drove my car up the driveway to where it narrows markedly with a steep drop off down to a pond on each side. I parked the car sideways right before the narrow part and left the doors wide open. If they somehow managed to get past that, the gate would stop them further up. God knows what it looked like to anyone driving past on the road. I have no doubt that it looked like crap.

I walked back to the minis in their garage feeling confident I had nipped the problem in the bud. I'd ignored the fact that they had been able to see what I was doing, which gave them time to formulate a plan. I opened their door and called for them to come out, saying, "Okay, girls. Time to run around. Stay in the yard!" Yeah. Like they were dogs or something. Misty knows she is far superior to a lowly dog, and I'm sure that comment made her more determined to foil my anti-mini horse escape measures.

Misty loose in the yard. Will I ever learn?

They muscled past me at the door and trotted out to the yard to eat. It didn't take long before I had a bad feeling about things. Misty was acting too suspicious, slyly glancing over to me every so often while her nose remained buried in the grass. I shrugged it off and settled down on the front steps to supervise them. Sunny seemed to be behaving herself. Misty was the one I was worried about as she pranced past and made her way to the snow fence near the pasture. First, she inspected it, then she pushed her nose against it. I noticed Sunny innocently looking up from her lunch, watching her. I swear they have telepathic communication with each other. By the time I turned back to look at Misty, she had already pushed her way under the fence, and all I saw was her backside as she cantered up the hill past the pole barn on her way to the neighbor's house. Before she disappeared in the distance, I yelled, "You'll be all alone, Misty! Hope you make it out alive with all the coyotes!"

I grabbed Sunny and put her back in the garage. I was so mad at Misty that I didn't run after her for once. She knew the way home—

she'd done the same thing enough times before. I wasn't going to play her game anymore. I sat back down on the step and tried to read for a while but couldn't concentrate. Suddenly, I heard a huge whinny coming from *the end of my driveway*. It was Misty. She couldn't get past the closed gate and was demanding that I march right up there and open it for her. That little brat was way too smart. She had run through the pasture to the neighbor's, then out their driveway and up the road to her own driveway. At least she knows where she lives.

I ran up there, huffing and puffing, and there she was. Her Highness was waiting for the lowly servant to open the gate for her. She pranced right through, head held high, and trotted down to the garage where Sunny waited, both of them probably laughing their fat little butts off at how Misty had pulled off the great escape.

Don't ask me why I continued doing this same thing over and over again. What's that quote from Einstein? "The definition of insanity is doing the same thing over and over and expecting a different result."

I guess that makes me certifiable.

The next episode was maybe a month later. I hadn't let them out for a while, but then I let down my guard. Once again, I closed the gate and parked my car sideways. I had come home from working ten hours on my day off. I wasn't in a very good mood but I let them out anyway. What could possibly go wrong? I sat on the front step eating pizza and soon realized they were gone. I gathered up the dogs, put them in the car, and went to grab the minis' halters, leads, and the bucket of grain, and away we went, four-wheeling in a four-door sedan out in the pasture. Every so often, I stopped the car, got out and whinnied at the top of my lungs, hoping they'd hear it and come running. They didn't do an answering whinny like they normally would. I grabbed the halters and bucket out of the car and walked the rest of the way down to my brother's house. Usually, I would find them there, eating his grass and leaving presents behind for him to find as he mowed his lawn. I'm sure he loved that, but he never mentioned it, maybe because it was free fertilizer. Unfortunately, the minis were nowhere in sight.

I went back to the car and the dogs and I drove up and down the gravel road, me periodically whinnying loudly out the window. I don't know if anyone saw me do that—I hope not—but at that point I was becoming really worried and didn't much care what I looked like. "Deranged" would be the perfect word, actually. And who knows what my dogs thought of all of it—it was a fun adventure for them, and they hung their heads out the windows and enjoyed the ride. I scanned the woods on each side of the road, looked up each driveway and into all the yards along the road. I didn't see the minis anywhere. The sun had set, and it was now almost full dark, and the horses were still gone. I drove home, a sinking feeling in my heart. *Where were they? Were they okay? Would I ever see them again?* I wondered.

I left their garage door open so they'd be able to get inside when they came home. *If* they came home. Before I went to bed, I went back outside and checked the garage. No minis. I tried to sleep but couldn't, and I finally got up around three in the morning and went outside to see if they were there. They weren't. Yes, I cried, and yes, I completely blamed myself. I went back inside and was able to sleep for an hour or two. At seven in the morning, I went to check the garage—and there they were! I ran over to them, burst into tears and hugged and kissed each in turn, bawling the whole time. "Don't ever do that again, okay? I thought you were gone for good. I thought you were dead. I was so worried! Thank God you're okay and found your way back home." I could tell they were worn out. They were acting somber and withdrawn, and the fact they allowed me to hug and cry all over them was unusual.

I never knew where they spent their night of freedom until years later. On one of our walks down the road, Breezy and I stopped to say hi to my neighbors, Bill and Laurie. They had been doing renovations on their house and garage. While we looked over the garage improvements, Bill mentioned that one night several years prior, they had been out in the garage with some friends, having a party or something, when they noticed two horses looking in the window at them. Yup. Misty and Sunny. Now I know where those little brats had been. They always did like his grass better. I suppose after window peeping, they grazed happily all night at his house and then, as dawn approached, decided they had better get their butts home or they'd be grounded. They were grounded all right.

Eventually, I settled on a new method of keeping them safe in the yard. I thought back to when I had bought a llama to keep the minis company when they were out in the pasture, plus to help protect them from the coyotes. He didn't work out, and when I found a new owner for him, that's when the minis moved from the coyote-infested pasture to their garage. I remembered that the llama breeder kept her huge male llamas in her yard by tethering them with a long, stretchy fabric lead attached to a big tire. I couldn't believe that would keep a 400-pound llama from running off, but she said it worked great. I had bought one of the leads, thinking I would use it for the llama, but never did. I figured if it was good enough for a llama, it would work for a mini horse, too, so I grabbed the lead and found a tire out in the pole barn. Since I had only the one lead and tire, I had to decide which mini was the best one to attach it to. I decided on Sunny since, believe it or not, she is the alpha mare. You'd think it would be Misty, but after long observation, I'd realized Sunny was the boss and, if she stuck around the yard, maybe Misty would too. You'd think I'd learn. Nope. Certifiable, remember?

One afternoon, I heard the sounds of a party from the nearest neighbors that I share the back pond with. They were hooting and hollering and having a great time. They had launched a rowboat, and kids were rowing back and forth across the pond.

The chickens were in the coop and were complaining that they wanted to get out in their outdoor run. I gave up and dropped whatever I was doing and let both the minis and chickens out to play.

This time, I hooked Misty to the lead and made sure the tire was securely attached. It had worked so well the last time with Sunny, maybe it would with Misty. Both minis grazed happily for about an hour, and I breathed a sigh of relief. Maybe this would be the solution.

I sat and read magazines while the minis enjoyed their lunch. The horses were doing fine until they wandered into the backyard and got spooked. They probably saw the boat through the trees and heard the people at the party. Suddenly, they were galloping around the house, Sunny in the lead, Misty close on her heels with the tire flying across the grass behind her. Before hooking Misty up, I had put a heavier tire on the lead, but it didn't slow her down a bit. They almost went up the driveway twice as I ran in pursuit. There was no way I could catch a speeding mini horse. Breezy joined in the fun and began chasing them, barking the whole time. I was yelling, "*Misty! Sunny! Dammit! Stop! Get back here! No! Son of a bitch! Misty!*"

The neighbors got an earful, like usual. I'm sure they'd heard much the same from my neck of the woods enough times that it didn't faze them. The minis galloped around the house, and Misty came down the hill in the front yard, the tire screaming along fifteen feet behind her. As she streaked past, I tried to grab the tire, but it was bouncing along way too fast. The minis did another circle around the house, and here they came again. Misty flew past me, and this time, I had to leap over the tire like it was a jump rope to avoid being hit by it as it bounced behind her.

They finally stopped to catch their breath and I pounced on the tire and grabbed Misty's lead. All of us were gasping for breath at that point. I carried the tire and lead rope and led her back to her garage, Sunny trailing behind as she followed us both inside. Once the door was shut, I put the tire down on the garage floor, then sat down on it and tried to calm them down. Eventually, they settled down, and I went to put the chickens back in their coop. It's a good thing that no coyotes had been in the neighborhood because that would have been a great time to nab a chicken dinner since I wasn't supervising them in their run.

I stumbled back to the house, went inside, and poured myself a huge glass of wine. So what if it was only three in the afternoon? I downed it in one go and then poured myself another one. I decided the tire wasn't a very good solution, so instead. now I halter up the minis and take them for walks down the road. Much less stressful. and as an added bonus, I get some exercise too.

## Chapter 24

# Raptor Rapture

Word has certainly gotten around in the local critter community about the free grub at my house. At first, it was the ducks. Then it was the geese. The turkeys soon showed up *en masse*. The crows decided to get in on the fun, as did the deer. And now? I have a red-tailed hawk swooping in nearly every morning to join the chow line.

When I'd step outside at the butt crack of dawn to fill the bird feeders and pour out some corn for the rest of the wild critters, I'd hear the strident call of a hawk somewhere nearby. When I'd finally spy it up in one of the oak trees, I'd tell it, "Go somewhere else, okay? I don't want you eating anybody." It would fly off with a plaintive cry when I walked toward where it was perched.

This went on each morning for at least a month. As time went on, I noticed the hawk would stay where it was, ignoring my pleas to not eat any of my bird buddies. It sat on its tree limb while swiveling its head and watching all the other animals digging into the bounty. The crows dive-bombed the hawk at first, trying to get it to leave, but eventually they shared the branch with the hawk.

Since I have absolutely no shame and have no problem making an ass of myself by loudly making every other kind of birdcall, I decided to try to speak Hawk: *Peuw Peuw Peuw!* When the hawk heard me, it immediately turned completely around on the limb so its back faced me while its body language so obviously screamed, *Lowly human, do not dare to insult me with your feeble attempt to imitate my magnificence.* It cracked me up when it turned its back on me, so I made a few more hawk calls to rile it up before calling it a day and going back in the house to locate my coffee cup and wake myself up.

As the days passed, the hawk continued to stay in the nearby trees while I was outside, which surprised me. I nearly fell over the day I saw it swoop down and land on top of the tarp-covered hay bales where I had been putting the crows' treats to keep the turkeys from gobbling them up. The hawk landing next to them caused the crows that had been eating to quickly scatter. That particular day, I had put out some mini hotdogs and leftover cheesecake for the crows. I love cheesecake, but I love it so much I will motor through nearly the whole thing, no problem. I decided to nip the problem in the bud and give the last few slices of cheesecake to the crows. They seem to like pretty much everything, so I figured that would be a nice treat. Not to mention that the temperature that day was below zero, so the fat and protein would help them stay warm.

Back inside the house, I watched out the window to see if the hawk was still on top of the hay bale. It was. I grabbed the binoculars to zoom in and see what it was eating, and I burst out laughing—it had an entire piece of cheesecake gripped firmly in its talons and was gobbling it with utter relish. Have you ever heard of a hawk eating cheesecake? I doubt it's ever happened in the entire history of the world. And it happened right in my front yard. It also dispatched a few of the hotdogs while the crows perched directly above it in the oak tree, cawing plaintively as they watched their breakfast being devoured. A couple of the crows landed on the hay bale behind the hawk and tried to steal hotdogs. That was entertaining to watch.

The next day, the hawk was already perched in the oak tree directly above the hay bale waiting patiently for me to appear with the food. It stayed there, watching me intently as I walked around the yard feeding everyone. It was only twenty-five feet up, and it allowed me to get closer than I could believe—until I tripped over my own feet, something I do with more regularity than I care to admit. It spread its wings, lifted into flight, and soared to the nearby woods. It must still have been watching me because it quickly returned after I finished putting out that morning's treat: freezer-burned chicken breast. Once again, it stood on the hay bale with a piece of chicken firmly grasped in its talons as it dug in.

Now every morning, when I'm awakened by the turkeys, crows, and other birds whining loudly for me to get my butt up and feed them, I have to put up with a hawk whining too. I kid you not.

I mentioned all of this to my friends, Tom and Mary, who are wildlife photographers in Alaska. They were surprised that the hawk allowed me to give it food. I decided that it's a really smart hawk—it saw everyone else getting free chow and not having to do any work for it and figured, *Why not?* and decided to join the gravy train.

One day, as I sat at my dining room table, I noticed Felix looking up from his cat bed in the bay window at something in the black walnut tree next to the house. Figuring it was a squirrel, I went to

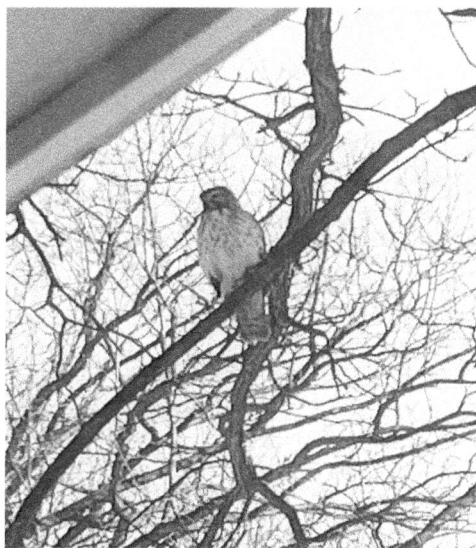

The hawk spying on me.

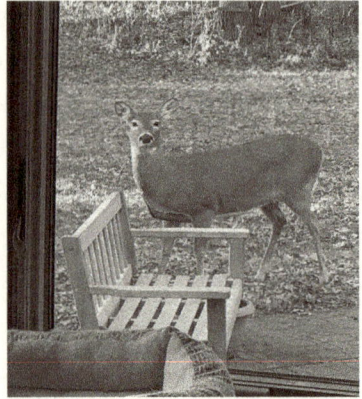

The turkeys and my deer friend, looking in at me from outside.

the window and looked up to see the hawk, in all its glory, peering down at me. The damn thing came to spy on me! Well, take a number and get in line, Mr. Hawk, because the squirrels, turkeys, geese, ducks, and deer all spy on me too.

I've never seen a hawk right next to the house like that, although several years ago a barred owl was in that same tree, looking in at Nutter and me. The squirrels have long snooped through the windows. What is it with these damn animals—are they voyeurs or something? Lately, the flock of turkeys comes to the bay window and looks in at me as I sit at the table working on my computer. The friendly doe does the same, pretty much begging me to come out and give her a treat. Next thing you know, a stinking coyote will sidle up and sneak a peek. It's like I'm living in a zoo, and the tables have been turned—the animals are outside looking in at me, the zoo animal. It's a seriously creepy feeling when I think of it like that. I used to joke that I wanted to call this place "Suzy's Zoo." Now I'm thinking "The Funny Farm" might be a better description.

## Chapter 25

# Talking Turkey

Sometimes, I wonder what in the hell I'm thinking when I do things—and whether I really *do* think before I do things. I'm not talking about the stupid stuff I've been known to do in my everyday life, although that would be another full-length book in itself. No, what I'm referring to is what I do when I interact with the wild animals around here. I've had people tell me that I anthropomorphize animals—meaning I attribute human characteristics or behavior to them as if they were people. Huh. *Really?* Yeah, I totally do that, and I'm not embarrassed to admit it. Well, not *too* embarrassed.

The only critters I don't treat like they are human are the coyotes. That's because they are pretty much the spawn of Satan, at least the ones around my house. No way am I ever going to think a coyote is capable of being cute and cuddly, much less friendly—not after everything I've been through with them.

I've mentioned a few times how I see so many similarities between the ways in which animals interact with each other and the ways that humans do with other humans. The only real difference

I can see is that humans are able to read and write and don't have built-in fur coats or feathers. Well...except for the guys with tons of back hair. Ugh. Oh—and we tend to overthink everything to the point of inertia. Animals know that only two things are important to survival: Are you a predator, or are you prey?

Peel back the thin veneer of "civilization," and we humans aren't that much different from what most of us consider lowly animals. And yes, the predator vs. prey applies to us, too, if you think about it. Not in terms of life and death, although in many parts of the world that definitely comes into play, but more in terms of power and control. Those who have the power are in control of the rest of us. However, they don't whack us and then eat us for dinner like an animal predator would. At least not yet, anyway. Thank God.

Here's a case in point of how I so often do things, *dumb* things, before my brain is able to send out an SOS telling me not to do what I'm already in the process of doing: The flock of wild turkeys had lately consisted of three older toms, four young jakes (immature toms), and two hens. This flock, or portions thereof, come to dine at the corn buffet several times a day, hang out in my yard, and snooze the afternoons away. The three older toms seemed to be best friends and always hung out together.

One morning, I noticed one of the three older toms (who I have since named Arthur) was alone and limping badly while making his way to the piles of corn by the bird feeder. He joined Agatha, a lone hen, who was already eating. His left ankle was badly swollen and looked either sprained or possibly broken. He kept his weight off of it as much as he could. I was only about two-and-a-half feet from both of them, which was the closest they'd ever allowed me to be to them. I wondered why he was alone and where his buddies were.

Soon enough, I noticed the other two toms he normally hung out with coming across the yard toward us. Arthur went to meet them. He hid his limp from them; in the animal world, you can't

Arthur the turkey.

show weakness. I've noticed the same thing with my chickens and birds—if they're sick, they'll hide it from the others as long as possible. Being seen as weak is a death sentence.

Suddenly, the two new arrivals ganged up and attacked Arthur. It was brutal. He was already in pain, and together they kicked his butt big time. This is where me doing stupid things comes in. I yelled at them from my spot near the bird feeder and then did something that you really should never do: I marched straight at the brawling turkeys while yelling, "Hey! Leave him alone, you assholes!"

The turkeys circled each other, spreading their wings and flying up to twirl and slash their spurs at Arthur. That really pissed me off. A little voice in my head was saying, *Uh...do you really think this is a good idea?* I ignored the voice and barreled right at the turkey fight, yelling at them the whole way.

The fight broke up, Arthur peeled off and the two aggressors backed away. "Leave him alone! Don't you dare hurt him!" There I stood in my yard, yelling at turkeys at eight in the damn morning. Unfortunately, it was spring, and the leaves hadn't yet grown thick enough to shield me from view of the road. Who knows who saw me? Or who *heard* me?

After my verbal lashing, the two toms slunk guiltily back to the pasture, and Arthur limped back to the corn while I stood there and remembered what a former co-worker used to say about me, "She's got balls so big she needs a wheelbarrow to carry them around." Yup. I certainly do.

Two years in a row, Arthur was booted out from his flock when spring rolled around. I have no idea why or what he did to deserve it, but the others bullied him unmercifully. Whenever he showed up, I gave him extra TLC and some of the good stuff—black oil sunflower seeds—for a special treat. Then I would hang out while he gobbled it up so I could shoo away the other toms that tried to chase him away. I no longer qualify as a crazy cat lady—now I'm a crazy critter lady. Whatever. If it makes me happy to make a poor outcast turkey happy, so be it.

I'd mentioned to my friend, Tom, the photographer who lives in Alaska, about how I had been feeding a flock of turkeys. He emailed me a video of turkeys fighting each other and told me I needed to watch the video because I obviously didn't know what they were capable of. I didn't have the heart to tell him that I already knew all about turkey fights, having inserted myself into a few of them. Not to mention the day the turkeys were peacefully eating as I stood among them when suddenly a group of toms that didn't belong to the flock came barreling from the pasture into our midst, and a massive fight broke out. Seven full-grown tom turkeys were duking it out right behind me. I didn't bother to turn around. The hen calmly pecking corn by my feet looked up at me as I said, "Men are dumb, aren't they?" I'm pretty sure she agreed with me. I turned and walked to the house, past the fighting turkeys.

So that you don't think this was an isolated incident in my ongoing interactions with the local wildlife, here's another doozy. Once again,

I was engaged in my daily activity of distributing piles of corn for everybody. Two out of the five deer that were lurking near the woods came running up to me and dug in. The turkeys soon showed up. Everyone was eating and happy. A job well done, I turned to go back to the house but noticed five tom turkeys harassing the tiniest deer. They spread wide their huge wings and chased after it, flying upward to scare it until it ran away. I marched in my fuzzy dog slippers all the way down to where they were and ripped those turkeys a new one until they de-puffed their feathers and began to look sheepish. "I won't put up with bullying!" I told them. "I won't feed you corn anymore if you keep that crap up."

The other deer were watching from the woods. I turned to the littlest deer and told it, "You know, you don't have to be afraid of them. What are they going to do? Peck you? Screw them. You're way bigger than they are. Run after them. Put the fear of God into them. You don't have to put up with being scared." I turned my back on the turkeys, went into the house, sat down, and only then realized I had gone up against five huge tom turkeys—alone. Turkeys that had no fear of an entire herd of much larger deer that towered over them. And there I was, berating them as if they were naughty children.

What I saw a few days later brought a smile to my face and gave me hope that the victims of the world can take back their power. The little deer that I gave the pep talk to? When the turkeys were chowing down on their corn, she galloped up to them and shoved them aside. It was freaking awesome. I would have gone out there to give her a high five, but that would have been too weird even for me. You have to give her credit—she heard what I said, and she acted on it. Okay, so I probably didn't have anything to do with her newfound courage, but it warmed my heart anyway.

Wild turkeys are really large birds—standing stretched up, toms can be four feet tall, with a wing span of almost five feet, and they can

The tiny deer after she kicked the tom turkeys' butts.

weigh more than 25 pounds, plus they can run up to 25 mph. And the spurs on their strong legs are potentially lethal. My Silkie rooster, Filbert, attacked me once. He flew up in the air, twirled, and sliced my face with his spurs. And he was only a foot tall and three pounds. Can you imagine what a full-grown turkey could do? The one thing I have in my favor is that the turkeys seem to have decided I am part of their flock. It has to do with how I interact with them, as well as learning what their vocalizations mean. I used to mimic their "*tuck tuck*" sound until I realized by observing them that it was their alarm call. No wonder they ran when I did it. Instead, they make a "*pew pew*" sound and also a purring noise, and those are the flock calls.

Yes, I'll admit it—I stand there in my front yard and make those noises to them. Well, it works. They haven't ganged up and killed me yet, and after I figured out that the alpha turkey was trying to dominate me, I quickly put a stop to that by dominating *him*— walking straight at him until he backed away while I hissed, "Do you really want to throw down with me? Huh? *Are you sure?*"

All of the things I've learned in my interactions over the years with my alpacas, llama, mini horses, and the goat, I now use with the wild animals. Except for the coyotes—nothing works with them. Except a 12-gauge shotgun. I can't believe I can say that because it's so against my values, but I reached my limit with them some time ago and realized there is no getting along with them here. They want to kill my pets and livestock and probably me, and I decided I wouldn't let them. We have reached a truce: as long as they leave me alone, I'll leave them alone.

What's really funny is that, as I sat here in my three-season porch typing this story, the turkeys came up to the house and looked in at me. "Yup, I'm writing about you," I said. "About the time when you were jerks and beat each other up." Two of the toms engaged in a mock fight for a few seconds, then continued on to the bird feeder. I swear to God, they can understand me.

# Chapter 26

# Sweets for the Sweet

Fall is mating season for the white-tailed deer, and they don't mess around when it comes to finding a paramour. One day in early November, when I was outside, something caught my eye. I stopped what I was doing and saw a handsome eight-point buck standing about thirty feet away and watching me. Since a buck in rut can be pretty much out of his mind with all the mating impulses flowing through him, I was a tad concerned. Not to worry—after a few moments of staring at me, he bounded away into the woods. I guess he decided I wasn't his type. Good thing, because the last thing I would want to do would be having nooky with a buck. I seem to have successfully dodged that particular inter-species bullet.

About an hour later, I noticed a familiar doe making her way up to the bird feeder, so I grabbed a couple of mini cinnamon rolls and went out to greet her. This was a different doe than the one I had made friends with the previous year. The new doe ran toward me because she knows when she sees me that there will be treats involved, and it turned out that she had a serious sweet tooth. One day, I had put out a stale lemon danish for the crows, but instead, this doe gobbled it down. I couldn't believe she would eat it, but after expressing an initial shock at the taste of lemon, she couldn't get enough of it. She also loved muffins—her two favorites were blueberry and pumpkin. One day in late fall I visited my neighbor, Ron, and he pointed out all the ripe pumpkins in his garden. He said he was leaving them for the deer because they love pumpkin. I replied, "They love pumpkin muffins too." I'm pretty sure he thought I was kidding.

Another doe and her fawn were also in the yard. Those two didn't trust me as much, so they tended to keep their distance. I tossed the cinnamon rolls to the first doe and she gobbled them up as the other two gazed longingly from afar.

When I glanced up, I saw that the buck was back. He had positioned himself about forty feet from us and his head was swiveling from one doe to the other while he tried his best to look rugged and handsome. It was obvious he was looking for some action. I turned to the two does to see what their reactions were—my doe ignored him completely and continued eating. She knew he was there, but she wasn't interested. Meanwhile, the other doe was prancing around with her tail flipped up onto her back, an obvious invitation. The little fawn had no clue what was going on.

I stood out there without a coat in the thirty- degree weather for fifteen minutes watching the drama unfold. When the fawn wandered over to the buck to say hello, I held my breath, worried

Mr. Tall, Dark, and Handsome posing for the girls.

that he would hurt it. The buck bent down to sniff the fawn and then charged after it a short distance to chase it away. This happened a couple of times until the fawn figured out that the buck wasn't his friend. For once in my life, there was no way I was going to get involved in that drama because the buck could definitely hurt me, either with his antlers or by running me down.

The buck turned his attention back to the two does. My doe was still ignoring him, but the other doe coquettishly flirted and tried to get him to choose her. I started laughing and said to all of them, "Oh my God, you guys—this is just like closing time at the bar when I was in my twenties!" Shaking my head and still snickering, I turned away to go back inside and warm up.

Soon enough, the daily visit by the two does and one fawn turned into a herd of six deer that visited my yard several times a day to check out the offerings. The friendly doe was the leader. I'd seen her around for a few years, so she was used to me. She was older and more experienced than the other deer who looked like they were yearlings, and that meant, as the leader, she had first dibs to snatch up all the treats and corn and, if any of the other deer attempted to nab something, she would shove them away and gobble up all of it. Several times I tossed part of a blueberry muffin over to the forlorn group, but before they could make a move on it, the doe was right there, hoovering it up.

She was smart, too—she figured out that if she didn't see me come out the front door or look out the living room window at the front of the house, she would circle around to the back of the house and look through the bay window until I noticed her. The turkeys had figured this out as well, and they'd stare in at me at all hours of the day. Whenever I saw the doe gazing in the window, I'd wave at her and say, "I'll be right out! Give me a second to grab your treat." She would wait patiently until I emerged with a muffin or other treat and tossed pieces to her.

At first, when I began feeding her treats, she would stay at least ten feet away from me and I'd toss the first piece to her. Then I'd toss the next piece five feet, then two feet. She would slowly come closer and closer because she really wanted her treat. Each day, we did the same thing until the day she came all the way up to me and ate the muffin from my hand before I could toss it. I was shocked and stood completely still so she wouldn't be startled. She kept a sharp eye on me the whole time, ready to retreat if I tried anything. I stared down at her in wonder. I never knew deer had whiskers on their muzzles and eyebrows like dogs and cats do. And long, luxurious eyelashes to go with their large, soulful eyes. She gazed up at me as she ate. When the muffin was gone, I held out my sugar-covered fingers, and she licked my fingers with her soft tongue. I was in shock that she trusted me so much. The other five deer were watching all of this happen but none were brave enough to come any closer.

Mrs. Deer sniffs my hand.

I've never really figured out the dynamics of a deer herd, so I can't tell you why they pal around together in groups, especially in winter, until suddenly they go off on their own. Rambo would know—he knows everything about anything critter-related. I think it has something to do with safety in numbers in the winter, particularly because of all the coyotes gunning for them. Plus, they can huddle together to stay warm when the temperature plummets to 8,000 degrees below zero. Okay, Minnesota doesn't get *that* cold, but it sure as hell feels that way sometimes.

That's why I wasn't surprised when spring rolled around and the herd of six deer dwindled down to only my friend, the doe. I called her Mrs. Deer—not exactly the most creative name I've ever come up with, by any means. Each morning, she would arrive bright and early, watching the windows and waiting for me to get up and come outside. The flock of turkeys usually awakened me with their gobbling and also when they would fly up onto my roof and stomp around. One morning, I woke up and heard a sole turkey gobbling right outside my window. I pulled back the curtains and looked out to see Arthur the turkey standing next to Mrs. Deer, both of them staring up at me. It was nice to see Arthur finally hanging out with somebody, even if it wasn't his own kind. I always felt so bad for him since his flock kicked him out every spring, and he trudged around all alone. He was such a sweet turkey and I don't know why they

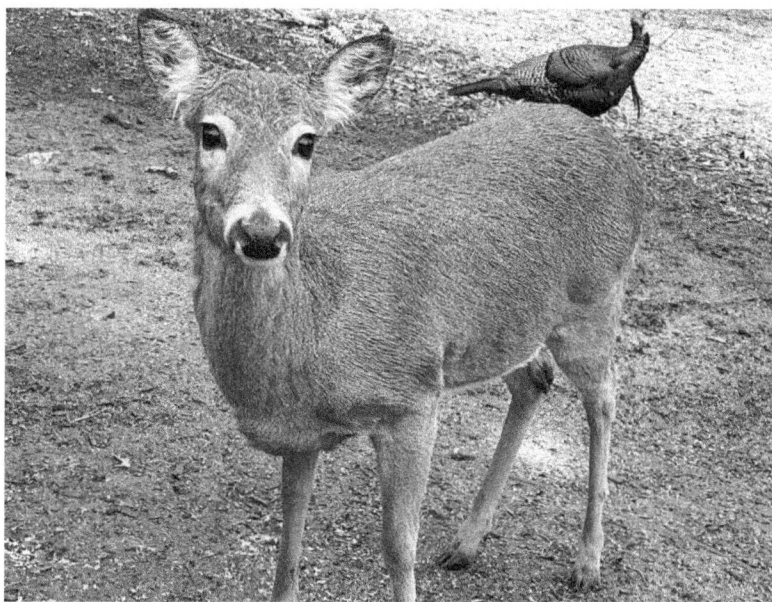

Mrs. Deer and Arthur.

treated him like crap. That's why I gave him a lot of attention whenever he showed up, and if the other turkeys arrived and tried to mess with him, I chased them away. I always root for the underdog...it doesn't matter to me if it's a turkey.

I went outside to feed Mrs. Deer and Arthur. She ate the corn out of my hand and let me pet her nose. Eventually, it got to the point that she allowed me to pet her head and neck. Deer fur is much rougher feeling than I thought it would be. I scratched behind her ears, which I think she liked. I wanted to take some photos of her, but I knew she'd be afraid of the phone, so I first let her sniff it and told her what I was going to do. Then, as she gobbled her muffin, I took a few pictures. She had become so used to me that next thing you know, she'll be inside the house, sitting on the couch, kicked back, and watching a movie. Stranger things have happened.

She trusted me but was wary when she saw anyone else, which was good. One day, I had a guy over to do some work on my house.

One of her favorites— a blueberry muffin.

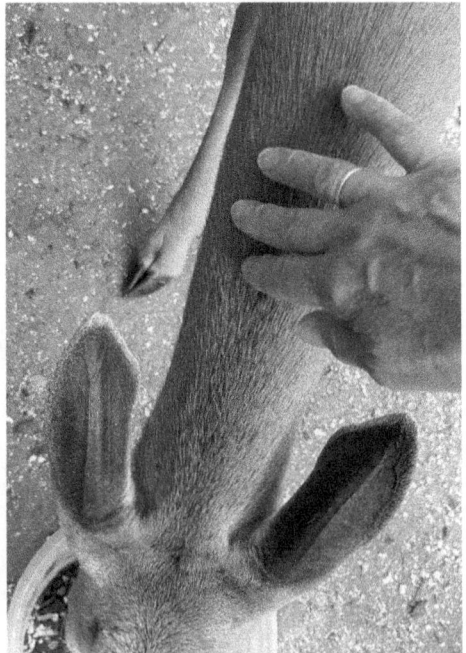

The first time she let me pet her.

He noticed Mrs. Deer in the yard, and we talked about how she would eat from my hand. It turned out he was as big of an animal lover as I am—he had chipmunks that he would hand feed. He named them Potato Chip and Poker Chip because that's the sound chipmunks make—*chip, chip, chip*. My friendly chipmunk never ate from my hand, but he usually came running when I made a *Chip! Chip!* sound. Yes,

Chippie stuffing his face while hanging out with me.

now I'm talking like a chipmunk in addition to making duck, geese, turkey, crow, hawk, and coyote noises. God help me. One morning, I sat atop my brick flower planter with my coffee and looked up to see Chippie sitting about two feet away, eating his sunflower seeds and hanging out with me. He was the sweetest little guy.

I never thought I'd make friends with wild deer and be able to interact so closely with them as well as with the wild turkeys, ducks, crows, geese, and the hawk. Although, I wouldn't say that the geese and hawk were necessarily friends, other than sucking up to me so they could get some chow. They all saw something in me that allowed them to trust that I meant them no harm. To be honest, I think it was because I treated them like they mattered—like they were individuals who had intelligence and sentience and weren't simply dumb animals like most people think they are. They aren't dumb. From observing and interacting with all of them, I now believe they don't act only on instinct—they are able to reason and make decisions based on what they experience. Mrs. Deer made a conscious decision to trust me the first time she approached me—I saw it in her eyes as she stared into mine. She thought through what could happen, what I might do, and consciously decided that I was no threat to her. In human parlance, she made a strategic cost-benefit analysis and decided the ROI was acceptable: *Okay, she might try to touch me, but in exchange, I'll get that yummy treat. Oh, what the heck...it's worth it!*

Sadly, not everyone shares my love of animals. One afternoon, Jay, the guy who plows my driveway in the winter, stopped by to chat and discuss the upcoming plowing season. I soon interrupted him as I pointed to the driveway, "Look! There's Arthur."

Jay turned to look and said, "I don't see a car. Wait...are you talking about that...*turkey?*"

"Yeah! That's Arthur. He's coming for his lunch."

"*You. Named. A. Turkey. Arthur?*" he enunciated slowly and with great precision, almost as if he was talking to a complete moron.

"Well, yeah, that's his name," I replied.

He tried to conceal his smirk as he turned away but I could see the expression on his face, and it practically screamed, *Boy, I cannot wait to tell the guys about this one!*

We all went to high school together, so unfortunately, they will know *exactly* who he's talking about. I was just glad I could provide some quality entertainment for him as I wandered off to get some treats for my buddy Arthur.

## Chapter 27

# Goose Down Smackdown

I'm not really a fan of geese, other than the handsome one I used to talk to on the road when his wife wasn't around. He was always polite and well-mannered. Most geese, however, tend to bite first and ask questions later. I'd been able to avoid being chased or bitten by any of the geese that showed up in my yard, but that was when only a few regulars stopped by. In addition to two of my favorites, George and Elsie (yes, I named some of the geese. Did you really expect anything different from me?), last spring, a huge flock of geese I'd never seen before began coming at all hours of the day. I don't know where they all came from, but one of them must have put the word out about the all-you-can-eat buffet, and everyone showed up to chow down. Each day, in addition to the regulars, at least fourteen additional pairs of geese could be found lounging around my front yard. I'm no math wizard, but even I can count up to a total of twenty-eight geese plus the regulars. I didn't trust most of the newcomers not to come after me, and I had to watch my back every time I stepped outside.

The turkeys were not at all pleased by this new development; they might have been as big as the geese, but they weren't as mean. The geese chased the turkeys away and hogged all the food. The poor turkeys were left to gather in a depressed huddle near the edge of the yard as they watched their feast being decimated by the ravenous flock of geese. If I tried to sneak some food to the turkeys, several geese would immediately come to investigate, and we were right back to square one. And, other than George and Elsie, I didn't dare turn my back on the rest of them.

One morning, George and Elsie showed up with a tiny baby. It was the cutest little ball of fluff I'd ever seen, and I decided to name her Addie. I congratulated them on the happy occasion and made sure to give them extra space so they didn't think I was a threat to their baby. Each day, they trusted me more to be near Addie. As they dug into their breakfast nearby, I'd sit up on the brick flower planter with my coffee and hang out with them. Each morning, the family would toddle up from one of the ponds, and it got to the point that, when Addie saw me, she'd run as fast as she could toward me with

Ralph and Agnes with three of their brood.

her tiny wings spread out because she knew I had the good stuff. You have no idea how cute a tiny little goose looks when running with its little wings flapping. I'd pour out some corn for her and then slowly back away so her parents didn't get nervous. I absolutely loved that little goose.

Another goose couple, Ralph and Agnes, soon had five babies trailing along behind them to the breakfast buffet. This family had obviously never been taught manners because not only did they bully poor little Addie, they tried it with me, too. They didn't trust me at all—until the day I saved their babies.

My vegetable garden was located close to one of the ponds, and all the ducks, geese, and other critters would traipse past it on their way up to the house for their daily tidbits. I had enclosed the garden with chicken wire that was haphazardly held up by plastic fence posts with mass quantities of zip ties holding the whole sorry mess together. Like so many of my other redneck creations, it looked like crap, but it got the job done. At least, that's what I thought until I noticed my favorite doe had absolutely no problem leaping over the fencing and chowing down on the succulent green beans and broccoli plants. I caught her in there red-handed on a number of occasions.

One day, Ralph and Agnes were outside the garden fence, honking loudly, flapping their wings, and frantically running back and forth. I ran down there to see what the problem was. I stood next to Ralph, the closest I'd ever been to him and probably not a good idea at the best of times, and asked him what the heck was his problem. That's when I understood why he and his wife were so frantic: all five of their babies were inside the fence while their parents were outside. The babies were darting here and there, peeping loudly and completely panic-stricken as they looked for a way out. I have no idea how they could have gotten in there. They were still quite small—about the size of my palm.

Ralph was freaking out big time. "Don't worry, you guys...I'll figure out how to save your babies," I told them as I circled around to the "gate," which is a polite term for my half-assed attempt at making an entrance into the garden. I pulled the gate aside and approached the babies who were piled up in the corner of the fence, peeping madly. When Ralph saw how close I was to them, he pretty much went ballistic. I was on the inside and he couldn't get to me, but it still scared the crap out of me because he was so out of control—and I still had to figure out how to get the little ones out.

I lifted the bottom of the chicken wire in the hopes that they'd see their escape route, but they were too freaked out by the big, scary human and ran back to their corner, screeching in terror. Ralph went more nuts and tried to attack me through the chicken wire. He was right in my face, biting at the chicken wire, slamming his body into it, and hitting it with his strong wings. I'm surprised the pathetic excuse for a fence didn't collapse on top of me. To my credit, I stood my ground and didn't back away as I told him, "I'm trying to help them. Let me help them, and quit trying to kill me!" Agnes was flipping out as much as Ralph. I reached down and scooped up one of the babies, which made it scream bloody murder. When Ralph saw me pick it up, he went right to DEFCON 1 and redoubled his furious attack on the chicken wire, trying to get at me and save his little one.

I took a deep breath and made my peace with God before I lifted the bottom of the fence right next to Ralph's snapping beak, quickly shoved the baby underneath, and watched as it darted away to join its parents. Somehow, I didn't get my hand bitten off. I had four more babies to go, and I expected Ralph to attack me each time as I shoved the next baby through. As I scooped up each baby, I marveled at how soft and fluffy they felt. I had no idea baby geese felt like that. Finally, all five were safe and nestled under Agnes, and both of the parents began to calm down. I sat down in the dirt, heaved a huge sigh, and said, "There, see? Your babies are fine. Thank you for not killing me."

After that, Ralph and Agnes trusted me and brought their little family near me on a daily basis. They knew I could have hurt their babies, but instead I saved them. I don't know the IQ of geese, but these two figured out that I wasn't the threat they had thought I was. I was in the good graces of two goose couples. That left the other fourteen pairs of newcomers to deal with, and they were far ruder and more ill-mannered.

This particular morning, I was in a rather foul mood because I hadn't slept much. Nutter had woken me up repeatedly by walking on my head. He likes doing things like that and seems to find it amusing, unlike me. I'm not sure why I didn't kick him out and shut the bedroom door, but I think I was too tired to even contemplate doing it.

After feeding the chickens, minis, and Donald, I made my way around the yard with the ice cream bucket of corn. Turkeys, geese,

This is only a few of the feathered mob. Notice how they are all watching me with their beady eyes...

and ducks were waiting with barely concealed impatience for me to get my ass over to them with the chow. The big flock of geese were being pushy, as usual. I wasn't in the mood to have any of them come near me and I told them to back off. A couple of them were being particularly annoying, and that's when I hissed, "I am *so* not in the mood for your crap this morning. You try anything, and I do mean *anything*, and I will wring your stinking necks and throw you across the yard. *Try me.*" One of the geese messed with a sweet hen turkey, and I took the ice cream bucket and smacked the goose on the ass with it. That was quite satisfying.

That day, I made it unscathed through the goose gauntlet. The next morning was another story. The flock's huge male alpha goose decided he was going to teach me a lesson for talking smack to the geese the day before. His wife and the other thirteen geese couples he hung out with were lounging in my front yard, arrayed here and there, watching me with beady eyes and barely concealed anticipation as I walked over to get some hay from the large hay bale. That should have been a red flag, but I ignored them. I was still holding the empty ice cream bucket and planned to put it on top of the hay bale while I fed the minis and Donald. I hadn't made it all the way over to the bale when some instinct made me turn around, only to see the big male goose racing toward me like a guided missile. I told him to back off but realized he was launching a full-scale frontal assault. He was planning to bite the living crap out of me and pummel me with his wings.

I threw the empty bucket, and it hit him smack in the head. That stopped him for a second, giving me enough time to pick it up and throw it at him again. Another head shot. I'm not usually that accurate, but he was only a foot or two away from me. I couldn't miss. As he retreated a few steps, the edge of one of his wings hit my arm, and that thing was like steel. That's when I got pissed. I ran straight at him and yelled, "Don't you *ever* try that again! I will *not* put up with that crap!" All the other geese were watching this go down, as were the turkeys, who I'm pretty sure, were happy about it because the geese were always so mean to them. I glanced at the other geese, and they seemed kind of shocked at seeing their fearless leader getting his ass handed to him by an old broad.

"I mean it, you little puke! I'm not going to put up with any shit from you!" He fluffed out his wings in defeat, then turned and slowly trudged away with his head lowered in shame. He may also have looked rather embarrassed because I took him down in front of everyone: geese, ducks, and turkeys. The crows and hawk may also have witnessed his utter humiliation. Typical bully. They're so brave until you stand up to them. Geese, people. All the same.

I'm sure word spread far and wide in the geese community about the huge smackdown: *Hey...did you hear? What's-his-face got his butt handed to him by an old lady. Yeah! You should have seen it. It was truly epic!*

He never tried it again, that's for sure. The other geese stayed the heck away from me, too. I don't back down. Screw that. The only thing I think I wouldn't go up against is a bear. When did I turn into such a huge badass? I guess I always have been.

Later, I noticed the turkeys mounting a counter-attack on the geese because they realized I was on their side of the battle. They had been sad because they thought the geese had replaced them as my favorites because they were getting all the food. No, the geese were simply being pushier.

## Chapter 28

# This Time It's War

In all the years I've lived here, the coyote situation has only become worse. I have no problem with them living out in the pasture or woods, but I draw the line when they repeatedly come right up to my house, wanting to kill my dog.

Like the other animals that come to my yard, the coyotes all tend to look alike and the only way to identify individuals is by their behavior. Yes, coyotes are all super-efficient killing machines, but most of them have some fear of people. When I'd go outside to chase them away, most of the coyotes would run, although they would circle back a time or two, hoping to get past me. I'd run at them again, and eventually they'd get the message and disappear into the pasture or woods.

Breezy detests coyotes, and they seem to hate her with an equal passion. Too many times to count, she'll leap up on the couch, look out the window, and launch into crazed barking when she sees or hears one outside. She runs to the front door, begging me to let her out to go after it. I grab her collar and push her aside as I dart out the door in full pursuit mode, chasing them away. Sometimes I forget to bring my baseball bat. They piss me off almost as much as they do Breezy. My friend Anita once said, "You're like a mama bear protecting your cubs." Damn straight I am.

This particular coyote started showing up this last spring. I'd noticed him skulking around the yard at all hours of the day, watching the bird feeders, sniffing the corn piles, and staring at the minis and Donald in their pen with homicide on his mind. Okay, in his defense, tons of potential food was there for the taking: birds, ducks, turkeys, geese, squirrels, miniature horses, and a goat. That's what happens when you feed the animals—you get other animals that want to feed on them. Add to that list Breezy when she was outside. All of that scrumptiousness was right there, waiting for him to select his next meal. You really can't blame him.

I figured the birds would be fine; he couldn't reach them up in the feeders. With so many squirrels around here, it would be a relief if he ate some of them. I did worry, however, about the ducks and geese. Particularly because the current goose family now included seven fluffy little goslings that came in the morning and early evening to eat corn.

One day, Breezy was going apeshit again on the couch, barking like mad. *Not again,* I thought. *This is the fourth day in a row!* Looking out the front window, I saw the coyote standing next to the nearby birch tree, gazing with rapt attention at the squirrels gobbling spilled birdseed under the feeders. He was way too close to the house, and I wasn't going to let that stand. "You have got to be kidding me," I muttered as I headed to the front door, tripping on Breezy several times as she tried to beat me there. Shoving her aside, I opened the door and stepped out onto the front steps in my floppy bunny slippers. Coyotes notice everything. He knew I was there, barely thirty feet away from him, but he acted like I didn't exist,

Two of the feral demon spawn at the edge of my yard at dawn.

which insulted me to no end. What, did he think I was no threat because I was almost sixty?

"Exactly what the hell do you think you're doing?" I asked it. "Get outta here!" It finally deigned to acknowledge my presence and ran a few feet. Emboldened, I walked out onto the patio. "GO!" I bellowed, and it ran toward the chicken coop and disappeared into the woods.

I had started hooking Breezy up to a lead so she could sit on the front steps and enjoy the day but not be able to run into the woods after the coyotes. I kept an eye on her periodically as I worked inside the house. She started barking, and I grabbed the baseball bat and ran outside to see her looking toward the nearby woods. Because I couldn't see anything, I walked in that direction. The damn coyote was there, staring with laser focus at Breezy. His teeth were bared, and he was definitely scary looking. Remember Jack Nicholson in *The Shining*? That image of him with the crazed eyes and feral grin? Yeah. That's exactly what the coyote looked like, except with fur.

He was trying to lure Breezy out there so he could kill her. Once again, he ignored me as I walked closer. "*Really?!* Didn't I tell you not to come back?" I ran toward him, waving the bat. He melted back into the woods and left. Good thing because I wanted to smash his head in. When did I become so homicidal?

Several weeks went by and I breathed a sigh of relief because I hadn't seen him around. Breezy was only allowed to be outside hooked up to the lead if I wasn't out there with her. She hated it because her favorite thing had always been to patrol the perimeter of the yard, looking for critters to chase. She had been snoozing on the front steps the last time I went to the window to check on her, and I went into the other room to work on my computer. Suddenly, I heard a choked off bark, and I went to investigate. The coyote had come back, and Breezy had tried to chase it, only to come up against the end of her twenty-foot lead. She could have broken her neck, and I absolutely should have known better. I saw the coyote not far away, his eyes alight with malice, his teeth bared.

I went to check on Breezy. She was coughing from her collar being pulled tight when she reached the end of her lead, but she was okay. I looked at the coyote and I saw complete and total red. I was so angry steam was probably coming out of my ears. The swear words were certainly coming out of my mouth.

"You dirty SOB. What in the hell are you trying to do? Kill my dog? We'll see about that," I snarled as I started toward the coyote. Once again, I ran after him, but this time, I had forgotten the baseball bat in my haste. Did coyotes think they were the only ones who could stalk someone? No thoughts were in my mind other than killing it with my bare hands—I was that angry.

The coyote ran to the backyard as I chased him but stopped on the small hill in the woods. There, he turned back toward me and stood, refusing to leave. By that point, I had stopped chasing him and started getting worried. He was facing me down, barely thirty feet away. I'd never seen one do that, and the look on his furry face scared me to death. I realized I was alone out there, clad only in my usual pajamas and fuzzy slippers, with no weapon. Breezy was still hooked up to her lead and was not in a position to back me up if the coyote decided to throw down with me. *Shit.*

The coyote looked past me to where he could see Breezy. He still wanted to go get her, and if he did, he would be coming right past where I stood. I tried everything that normally works to get rid of coyotes: I yelled, I waved my arms, I swore at it. Nothing had any impact whatsoever; the thing didn't care. I was a non-entity, and I didn't matter in the least. I was no longer mad; I was petrified. I cast around by my feet, looking for something to protect myself with. All I saw were some leftover oak logs that my brother had split years ago and never bothered to come get. I reached down, grabbed one, and hurled it toward the coyote. It didn't flinch. I grabbed another and another. Still no response other than a quick flick of its eyes toward me. With a sinking feeling, I realized that this could finally be the day I might have to fight a coyote with my bare hands. All these years, I've talked big to the coyotes, telling them they were no match for me, *blah, blah, blah.* But when it finally came down to it, I realized I was impotent in the face of their greater strength, speed, and cunning, not to mention this coyote's sharp teeth, which were on full display. And believe me—that was a terrifying thing to realize.

One more time, I hurled a log at him and screamed at the top of my lungs. He must have been sick of listening to me because he turned and stole into the underbrush. I was shaking with fear by that point and knew I had to get back to the house, but no way in hell was I going to turn my back on that thing. I ended up walking backward the entire way to the house, praying that I didn't trip and fall on my ass. Because with the way those things can move, he would be on me in a nanosecond, ripping my throat out.

I unhooked Breezy and brought her inside, where I collapsed on the couch and caught my breath. My blood pressure was through the roof. Eventually, I calmed down enough to send an email to Rambo with the blow-by-blow account. He quickly responded by saying he was coming over with a 12-gauge shotgun and would show me how to use it. Good old Rambo—he doesn't mess around.

When he and his wife arrived with the shotgun, we stood next to the minis' pen as he showed me how to load the shells, where the safety was, etc. I fumbled with it and dropped a few shells on the ground as I tried to load them. "Oops…will they blow up if they hit the ground like that?" I asked.

"No, they're okay," Rambo replied, grimacing at my incompetence. "But you need to figure out how to use this thing before I leave." I continued loading and unloading shells. I could tell he didn't have a lot of confidence in my skills and probably thought I would never be able to master it. He gave me two kinds of shells. One kind was blue. "Those will put a world of hurt in the coyote," he said. The other was red. "Those kind will end that thing," meaning kill it dead. His wife offered me encouragement; she seemed to think I could pull this off. Rambo, big game hunter extraordinaire, wasn't so sure.

After they left, I put the unloaded shotgun in a closet in my house, with the shells separate. I was scared of the thing. Back in the early 1970s, my brother and I used to go out in the pasture and shoot trap so I'd used guns before. Back then, he said I was faster than him, and I was good at blasting the clay pigeons out of the sky. But I hadn't shot a gun at a moving target since I was fourteen. Now, at almost sixty, could I pull it off? Good lord, I can barely kill an ant because I feel bad for it. How would I be able to take down a big animal like a coyote?

I found out soon enough.

Dawn was painting the sky to the east with pastel colors as I poured corn into the bucket, ready to go outside to feed everyone. I was about to open the door when I heard the geese making an unholy racket, honking loudly. As I stepped outside, I saw the coyote running near the front pond with a baby goose hanging limp in its mouth. It streaked into the woods and was gone. I ran outside all the way down to the pond to check on the rest of the goose family. The coyote was long gone, and the geese were in the pond, close to the water's edge, panicking. One of their babies had been snatched away and was dead. I stood there, feeling helpless, and told them how sorry I was. Then I remembered the shotgun. I looked at the geese and declared, "I'm going to kill that bastard. Your baby didn't die in vain. *I have had it. I'm done.* That son-of-a-bitch is gonna be dead."

I stalked back to the house, pissed beyond measure. I went straight to the closet, grabbed the gun, and went to grab two shells. I debated between the blue "world of hurt" and the red "kill it dead" but finally chose the blue. I still wasn't sure I could do this, but I wanted to be ready just in case. I set the unloaded shotgun and shells near the front door and went to make a cup of coffee.

About an hour later, Breezy leaped up from her nap on the couch and barked like a maniac. I rushed to the window and saw that the same damn coyote was back. It wasn't enough that he had eaten a baby goose for breakfast, now he was out by the corn piles near the minis' pen, looking for another tidbit.

I ran for the steps on my way to the front door and fairly flew down them. I didn't know how much time I had, but I was going to go out there loaded for bear. Or coyote. I grabbed the gun and shells, along with my hearing protector earmuffs, and went outside. The coyote spotted me and darted around the back of the minis' garage. I stood on the steps and loaded one shell into the gun with shaking fingers. Ha! I managed it fine. Take that, Rambo. I stood on the front step, wondering if the coyote would break cover. I noticed three turkeys hanging out on the hill between the minis' garage and the house. I figured I'd know if the coyote was heading their way if they got nervous.

It didn't take long. The turkeys looked to their right, then took off for the woods. And there he was, bold as day. He saw me standing on the steps, shotgun in my arms. I sighted it on him but was worried that if I stood where I was, the shotgun pellets might hit my car or the metal roof next to the garage and ricochet. Who knows, but at least I was thinking. I stepped down a bit lower and sighted on him again. He had now sat down on his haunches and was staring right at me, a huge, leering grin on his face. He seemed amused. He probably was. He had messed with me enough and won each encounter to that point. If coyotes can laugh, that's what he was doing. It was not normal coyote behavior.

I sighted on him again, then remembered the gun's safety was still on. *Crap!* I lowered the gun, found it, and disengaged it. I don't know why, but that coyote was giving me all the time in the world. I sighted on him again. I still had no idea if I could actually do it. The coyote continued watching me but got bored and rose to leave. He started away to my right and would soon disappear from view behind the side of the house. I wouldn't get another chance.

I somehow remembered from shooting clay pigeons years ago that the only way to hit them when they're moving fast is to lead them with the gun. Aiming the shotgun, I tracked ahead of the coyote. He was almost to the edge of the house. Before I knew what had happened, the gun went off with a huge blast. I didn't remember pulling the trigger. I didn't make a conscious decision to do it. My body took over and did it. And I nailed that sucker. I hadn't shot a moving target in over forty-five years and I got him dead to rights.

After lowering the gun, I remembered it was only seven in the morning on a very quiet summer day. *Everyone* had to have heard the gun blast. This area is pretty much still rural, but the city frowns on shooting out here and only allows bow hunting. *What if someone decided to call the cops?* I thought as I darted into the house and ran to hide the shotgun back in the closet. I hid the box of shells in another closet. I went over to Breezy on the couch and told her I had taken care of the coyote problem for her. I went and sat at my computer and waited in fear for the cops to show up. How was I going to explain it if they knocked on my door? My hands were shaking like a leaf. I could not believe I had done it. I didn't feel good about having done it. But I felt like I *had* to do it. The coyote had escalated far past the point where it was safe for my animals or me, for that matter. For him to have sat down and watched me as he did was beyond abnormal behavior for a coyote.

An hour passed, and the SWAT team never showed up to kick down my door. My hands were no longer shaking, and I wrote an email to Rambo telling him what had happened. I'm sure he was shocked to the core that not only had I managed to load the gun correctly after my earlier fumbling attempts, but I had hit my target on the first try. I think he was proud of me, though he would never come right out and say it.

He and his wife soon drove up and he went to deal with what was left of the coyote. A few weeks later, on one of our walks, Breezy and I stopped at Bill and Laurie's. I told them all about it. They both said, "Yeah, we heard a gun going off that morning and were wondering what was going on." Laurie high-fived me and said she was going to get a shotgun, too, because the coyotes had been in their yard menacing her dog. I haven't heard any gun blasts from her neck of the woods yet, but it's only a matter of time. She's tiny but fierce. Between her and me, the coyotes have no idea what they've unleashed upon themselves.

## Chapter 29

# Feline Fine

Once again, October was acting like winter. It was only seventeen degrees outside. Even for me, someone who loves winter, it was a slap in the face for it to be that cold so soon. The turkeys were already milling around in the predawn chill, so I bundled up and brought out birdseed for the feeders and cracked corn for the turkeys and crows. The chickadees were frantic as I filled up the bird feeders. One landed on the feeder right next to my head. After filling all of them, I went down to the driveway to deposit several mounds of corn. Fourteen turkeys came running and dived in. Next up was bringing hay to Donald and the minis. Once everyone was fed and happy, I went back inside the house where it was blissfully warm.

I filled up my coffee cup and glanced out the kitchen window at the eight inches of snow that had fallen. I like snow, but this was too damn early—it was a record snowfall for that early in October. Among all the critter tracks in the snow, I noticed some new ones from overnight on the snow-covered landscape rocks alongside the house. The tracks led out between the black walnut and birch trees and then on to the back woods. I knew they weren't dog tracks as Breezy hadn't been out there. I figured it was a coyote, which made me mad if it was right next to the house like that. I decided I might as well bundle up again and go out to feed the chickens. But first, I would investigate the tracks.

I opened the front door to see that the turkeys had already hoovered up all the corn, so I brought out more, plus leftover beef stew for the crows. Yeah, I know, but I figure it's better than throwing it out. And the crows seem to love my cooking, plus the turkeys won't let the crows have any corn. I know the turkeys won't eat the meat, so the crows will get breakfast too.

Heading to the back of the house, I bent down to look more closely at the tracks. They weren't coyote. I'd learned a few years ago from a guy who runs a wild animal sanctuary what the differences were between coyote tracks and other kinds, like cats. Not house cats…I'm talking bobcat and mountain lion. I watched this guy walk into a cage with a full-grown mountain lion and pet the damn thing. He knew his stuff. He said that coyote tracks would show claw marks. Cat tracks don't—just the paw itself. Well, wasn't that great, because the tracks next to my house *didn't have claws.*

My mom had seen a bobcat here probably thirty years ago, and my friend Bridget spotted one hanging out at the waterfall garden next to her condo a few years ago. *In town.* Other people in her condo had also seen it, so she

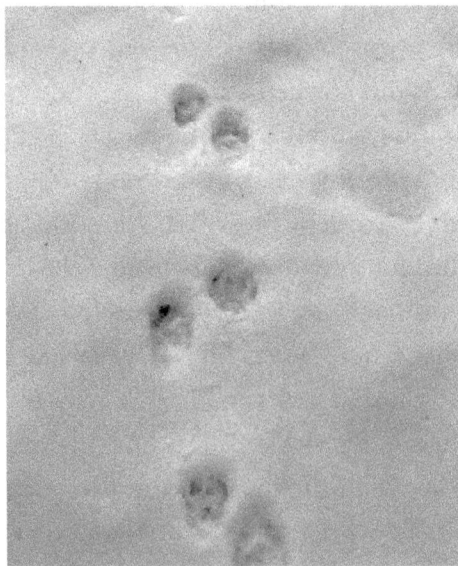

Bobcat tracks in the snow.

wasn't hallucinating. Yes, bobcats live around here. I've never seen one, but in the woods, I have heard snarls and other vocalizations that sound like the ones I find when I go on YouTube looking for "bobcat snarls."

I took photos of the tracks with my phone and a few more with my hand next to them to gauge their size then went to feed the chickens. I noticed that the damn mice had managed to push out the piece of wood I'd jammed in the hole they'd made in the coop wall from outside. I'd found baby mice floating lifeless in the chicken's water dish, so I knew they were coming in from somewhere. Now, I'd have to patch that hole because, if it was a little bigger, a mink would have no problem sneaking in and decimating the flock. One more thing to do. Yay.

Back at the house, I grabbed the tin snips, a hammer, and metal staples and went back to fix the hole. I had to stumble through the underbrush to get to the back side of the coop where the hole was. Luckily, the nearby chicken run had quarter-inch metal hardware cloth, and I cut enough of it to cover the hole. I squatted down to hammer in the staples that would hold the hardware cloth to the side of the coop. Let me mention that I had barely been up for half an hour and had absolutely no coffee in me yet, and I was still in my pajamas. My fingers were cold, and I had, of course, hit them a few times with the hammer. My parka was too bulky so I took it off and threw it on the snow. I was beginning to get annoyed. Yes, I was cold, but I was pissed too, which will keep you warm. Plus, I'm a Minnesotan. We laugh in the face of the cold.

I finally finished and gathered up the tools and my coat. My fingers were freezing and the rest of me wasn't too far behind. Stumbling through the brush, I made it back to the house. The turkeys were now in the backyard, the second round of corn long gone. I sighed and went back inside the house to warm up, look at the photos I'd taken of the tracks, and research them on the internet.

An hour later, I was 100 percent sure it had been a bobcat. Not only did the paw prints match what I found online, but the way it walked was the exact same, too. The size of the prints was about two inches—definitely bobcat size, and thankfully not mountain lion size. And yes, mountain lions have been spotted along the Minnesota River nearby. A month prior, one was run over by a car on a freeway not that far from where I live. Close enough for a mountain lion to cover in less than a day.

Next, I wanted to see what a regular cat paw print looked like next to the bobcat's. I grabbed my fourteen-year-old cat, Nutter, and went out the back door. I didn't bother with a coat since we wouldn't be out there long. He was wondering what the heck was going on. One minute, he'd been snoozing in his cat bed in the warm sun in the bay window; the next minute, he was out in the freezing cold. The turkeys were still out back, probably also wondering what I was doing.

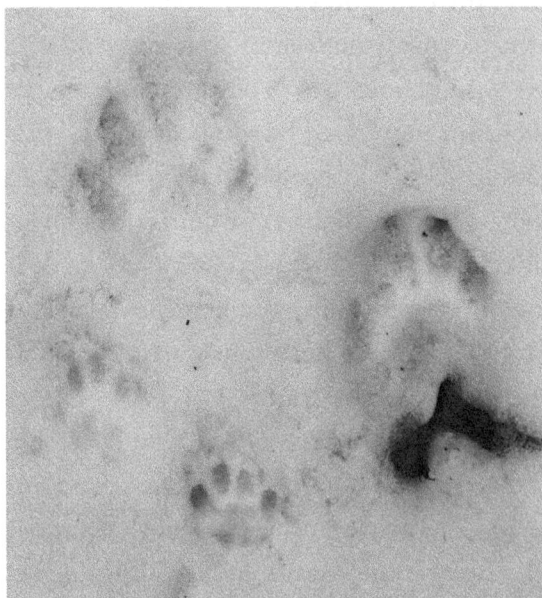

Nutter's pawprints compared to the bobcat's.

I slogged out in the snow and found a good paw print and set Nutter's foot down next to it. I lifted him back up in my arms and took a photo of it. I found an even better set of prints—two paw prints next to each other. I put Nutter down with his paws in the same positions next to the bobcat's. I have to give it to Nutter—he didn't complain at all about having his warm little feet jammed into the cold snow. Having known me for fourteen years, he is fully aware that I tend to do odd things.

Back inside, I set him back down in his cat bed and gave him a treat to make up for what he'd gone through. I pulled up the photos on my phone and sucked in my breath. Holy crap. Nutter's paws were *tiny* compared to the other ones. Of course, I had to email them right away to Rambo and tell him I now had undeniable proof that bobcats were around. I'd been telling him for years that I'd heard them, and he'd always scoffed. This time, I had proof. I'm still waiting for him to admit he was wrong but I haven't heard a peep out of him. It's exactly like with the bear—I had told him over the years that a bear hung around here. He never believed me…until the day he did.

A month or so after the paw print episode, a dusting of snow fell overnight. It had been a weird winter—tons of snow in October, and then November fizzled out and seemed to think it was mid-September weather-wise. I pulled back the living room curtains in the early morning and glanced out to see if I needed to fill the bird feeders or if it could wait a while. In the snow were tracks that could be either coyote or bobcat. It was bugging me, and so I went outside to examine them, wearing no coat. Tons of tracks were under the feeders and leading down to the driveway to where the corn feed takes place. I followed the tracks, and they looked to me like bobcat, not coyote. A few deer tracks were here and there, but not many. Walking up the driveway, I continued following the tracks. They went both directions on the driveway and also went down the steep hill to the open water near the pond's culvert. The tracks were smaller than a coyote's, plus they didn't show any claw marks. I measured my hand against them and they were the right size—definitely bobcat. At one point in the driveway, the gravel had been dug up and kicked backward—it looked like the bobcat had dug in his paws and launched into a run, chasing something.

I thought about taking more photos, but what's the point? Rambo didn't believe me the other times I told him there was a bobcat here. I was freezing by then, so I went back in the house and immediately fired off a text to Rambo. He would usually have been hunting out in my pasture, but he hadn't shown up that morning. I could have shown him the paw prints and proved to him once and for all that I wasn't hallucinating.

I was pretty sure there had been a black bear skulking in the thick woods near the pond. I'd never seen Breezy act like that. She ran toward the woods, growling, then she stopped and jumped straight backward, never turning her back on whatever it was. She did this several times and I noticed the fur was raised on her back. It couldn't be a coyote or raccoon because she'd have gone full throttle after it. This time, she wasn't sure, and she's normally fearless, plus she was looking higher up than she would if it were a coyote.

I yelled for her to stop and come back to the house. Thankfully, she's finally learned to listen. I had been dragging the garbage bags to the car to drive them up to the garbage cans by the road, and now I wondered if it was safe. I put Breezy in the car and shut the door. Then I went back to the house to grab a baseball bat. I'd lost track of where my favorite bat was, but this fifty-year-old scarred and gouged wooden bat would work. Why I thought a measly little bat would hold up against a huge bear, I'm not sure. Obviously, I wasn't thinking clearly. Like usual.

It was getting dark as I put the rest of the garbage bags in the trunk of the car and drove slowly up the driveway, looking in the woods to see if I could spot anything. The sun was lowering in the west and was in my eyes as I looked to my left, blinding me. Plus, with the tons of brush and buckthorn in the woods, I really couldn't see if anything was stalking me. I stopped the car at the end of the driveway and grabbed the bat, gripping it tightly as I walked over to retrieve the garbage cans and drag them to the end of my driveway. Of course, they were stored right next to the woods—the same woods where something huge and furry might be lurking. *What the hell*, I thought. *It can only kill me once.* At least Breezy would start barking if she sensed it, so I'd know the end was near.

I dragged the cans down to the road, went back to pull the garbage bags out of the car, and loaded them into the cans, watching the woods the whole time and keeping a keen ear for any noises. Once everything was loaded in the garbage cans, I darted back to the car, jumped inside, and quickly locked the door. Heaving a huge sigh of relief that I was still among the living I turned the car around, and we made it back to the house and safely inside.

I had to immediately text Rambo to let him know. He didn't believe me. He never does.

Breezy acted weird another time. She refused to get off the steps when I took her outside one night to do her thing. I couldn't convince her to follow me to the yard. She is *never* scared. She decided she would rather hold it all night long than go out in the yard, so that tells you something.

Later that summer, I was feeling brave and went for a walk alone out in the pasture and surrounding woods. I never do that anymore because of what might be lying in wait for me out there. When I was a kid, I spent hours alone out in the pasture nearly every day, wandering around, even in the dead of winter. For whatever reason, not as many scary animals lived around here back then. A skunk or fox was the extent of it. No coyotes, no geese, no bald eagles. The coyotes didn't show up until I was in high school in the late '70s, and the geese maybe ten years before that. It was a big deal when the geese first landed in one of our ponds. My brother and I ran out to look at them when we heard them honking. We'd never seen them before and had no idea what they were. Now, every manner of critter under the sun has taken up residence around here. I suppose because they don't have anywhere else to go, with all the development that has occurred in nearly every direction except where I live.

As I walked along the mowed trail that led down to the neighboring house, I noticed a pile of weird animal droppings. A big mound of what looked like berries had been deposited right in the middle of the trail. I didn't think much of it, deciding it must have been a goose with diarrhea. After wandering around the pasture for a time, I went back to the house and headed up the driveway on my way to visit the front part of my property. Huh. The same kind of droppings were also on my driveway. *That goose must have really gotten around*, I thought.

I completely forgot about all of it until the day Rambo came out to set up trail cameras in his happy place out in the pasture. He likes to reconnoiter the entire property, and he came back to the house by way of the trail where I had seen the droppings. I was sitting out on the front patio with Breezy when I saw Rambo practically running toward me from the pasture. I have never seen him run, so I knew something was up.

He could barely speak in full sentences because he was so excited. I finally understood what he was saying as he stumbled over his words: "Bear! You have a bear!" *Well, gosh, Rambo. Tell me something I didn't know*, I thought. *You're the one who didn't believe me all these years.*

He had seen the same droppings on the trail—it was bear scat. He knew what it was because, well, he's Rambo. He hunts everything under the sun. He knows his critter poop. The berries in it were buckthorn berries. No wonder it looked so gross—buckthorn berries have a laxative effect.

A few days later, I was feeling brave again, and I walked back on the trail and looked at that pile of berries. Yuck. That was certainly a large pile. I went back in the house and googled "bear scat" and for good measure, "bobcat scat." Yes, that was definitely bear scat.

Hmmm—I had always thought it was a raccoon that had been bending the heck out of the metal poles that hold my bird feeders. I'd get up in the morning and they were bent to the ground. Could a 40-pound raccoon bend that metal? Or was it a bear? I don't think I want to sit outside at night and wait to find out.

## Chapter 30

# Fight Club

One evening in spring, I heard what sounded like two raccoons in a knock-down drag-out fight. Snarling, with body-slamming thumps, kind of like a WWE cage match. I went into the porch to investigate. *Where was the noise coming from?* I wondered. I looked out to the backyard but still couldn't tell. Always wanting to be prepared in case of a wild animal incursion, I grabbed the baseball bat from its handy location next to the back door and looked both ways before stepping outside. I walked around outside the porch, but that wasn't where the noise was emanating from.

Huh. It seemed the noise was coming from inside the porch—between the porch ceiling and the roof.

I quickly realized it wasn't raccoons but squirrels. I walked further into the yard and turned back to look at the house. A lone red squirrel stood on the roof peak, near a hole that they had chewed into the attic through the two-by-four wood trim. It was wringing its hands…paws… whatever. With a concerned look in its eyes, it was gazing, like me, toward the source of the noise.

Squirrels usually run as soon as they see me, but this one didn't. It looked at me. I looked at it. "What the heck is going on in there?" I asked it. "Are they having a domestic or something?"

Having not received an answer from the paw-wringing squirrel, I went back inside the house. The noise continued unabated; angry squirrel talk was interspersed with banging noises. I tried to concentrate on what I was doing on my computer, but it was too noisy. I stalked back into the porch, grabbed the baseball bat and isolated the likely source in the ceiling. I then firmly bashed the fat end of the bat on the ceiling. "Hey! Keep it down, will ya?" Nope. They carried on. *Bang!* I smashed the bat harder. "*That's enough!* Shut the hell up already!"

That finally did it. The noise stopped. I laughed later when I thought of the expression on the face of the outside squirrel. It was so funny, kind of like it was thinking, I *don't know what to do. What should I do? It sounds like they're gonna kill each other in there. Do I need to call the cops? I'm sure as heck not gonna get into the middle of that one, no sirree! I'll stay out here where it's safe.*

Another day, another squirrel drama. Breezy shot out the front door, her target a red squirrel, which she chased into a section of gutter downspout that was lying where I had left it on the patio. She ran from one end to the other trying to flush out the squirrel. I stood on the steps by the flower planter and watched the excitement.

She'd done this same thing in the past and had tons of fun. I'm not sure what the squirrel thought of it, though. Suddenly the little guy darted out from the end nearest me and stood in the wide open, fully exposed. Breezy was still staring with laser focus at the other end. The squirrel saw me, looked back over its shoulder, and saw the dog. It stopped there, frozen. *Oh no! What do I do now?* was written all over its little rodent face.

Breezy noticed it right about then and was readying herself for pursuit. I yelled to the squirrel, *"RUN!"* It burst into motion, leaped over the brick flower planter, catching air the entire way, right past my face. I screamed as it hurtled past my nose in a blur. Breezy pursued it down the steps to the large evergreen tree next to the house. The squirrel made it! Up the tree it raced, onto the roof, and off to points unknown, probably my attic, shitting bricks the whole way, I'm sure.

This has now become my new form of entertainment: *"RUN!"* I yell at the squirrels gathered around the bird feeder before I let Breezy outside and, hearing my warning, they scatter in the wind. Breezy has outsmarted me a few times and shoved the storm door open before I could warn the squirrels. I watched one of those times as they darted away in all directions, and Breezy actually caught one next to the birch tree. She proceeded to shake it like a chew toy. It sounded like one too. *Squeak! Squeak!*

I held my hand to my mouth in horror, wanting to save the squirrel but thinking it was too late. I hid like a coward behind the door. I could not watch. "Oh no, it has *got* to be dead," I muttered and peeked back outside. No, it was lying there on the ground next to the birch tree, staring at me in accusation. Breezy, for some reason, was ignoring it, I suppose because it quit squeaking.

After I got Breezy to come in the house, I said a little prayer for the squirrel. Later, I looked outside, and it was gone; somehow it lived. I'm pretty sure it's still coming to the bird feeder. Fool. And Breezy is still chasing all of them.

The red squirrels had figured out a way to get into my attic and also above my porch, entering through a small hole in the eaves. If I could get up on a ladder—and not lose my balance and fall onto my head—I would fix the hole myself. I need to hire someone to remove the squirrels and repair the hole. I can't allow the furry varmints free rein to run rampant up there.

One night, I was awakened by the most god-awful noise. One of those evil little bastards was up to something in the attic. I looked at the clock, and it was 3:30 in the morning. I groaned. The noise continued. I threw off the covers and stomped out of my bedroom. *Where the hell is that noise coming from?* I wondered. Walking up and down the hallway, I echo-located it like a dolphin. *There! The little bastard was right there!* I stood under the attic access panel. The demonic creature was trying to find his way into the house. I envisioned rolling over in bed and coming face-to-face with a furry rodent face leering at me. First a mouse, then a snake—why not a squirrel? I had to do something about the situation. No way was I sleeping with a squirrel.

I grabbed one of the kitchen chairs and positioned it under the attic panel. What I was doing clambering up onto a chair in the middle of the night, half asleep, I don't know. I reached up with my arms but couldn't touch the ceiling. I made it back to the floor without falling on my face and commenced pounding on the nearest wall. The squirrel noise stopped momentarily and then started back up. I pounded again, same result.

Now I was getting pissed. How could I get that thing to stop? I grabbed a broom out of the closet and stood under the spot. "Quit it, you damn thing! I've had it!" And I rammed the broom handle up into the panel. *Boom! Boom!* Momentary silence then the squirrel went right back at it. "Stop it! Don't make me come up there and kill your ass!" I yelled. My two cats, who had been watching my shenanigans from a safe distance down the hallway, scattered.

The sheer gall of the creature was maddening. I gripped the broom handle like I was choking the life out of it, like I wanted to do to the squirrel, and rammed it as hard as I could up into the wood panel, which lifted about a foot. Insulation rained down on my head as I turned the air blue, swearing at the squirrel.

Silence, finally. I stood there for about five minutes, waiting, just waiting, for that little furry bastard to start in again. He didn't. I had finally put a stop to it. I shook the insulation out of my hair and went back to bed, but couldn't sleep because I was dreading the noise starting again. At least I was snug under the warm covers. Alone.

Several days later, my friend Bob came over to fix the old Ford tractor that my brother had left in the pole barn when he moved. Along with tons of his other belongings, by the way, but we won't go there. Bob noticed a red squirrel running along my roof and then darting into the hole in the eaves. "Sue! You have a red squirrel in your attic!"

"Yup, I know." That may have been uttered in a long-suffering type of intonation. An *I-give-up-what-the-hell-can-I-do-about-it* kind of voice.

"You have to get rid of it! Those things are bad news. I hate those damn things."

"Yeah, but how do I get rid of them? I tried a live trap once and they stood on top of it and left walnut shells to taunt me."

"They're smart little bastards, no lie. You need a pellet gun."

"Or a .22," I said, referring to a .22 caliber rifle. That would put the fear of God into them. At least before they disappeared into a cloud of vaporized fur. I smiled, thinking of it. Me, the animal lover, contemplating extreme violence shows how far those things have pushed me. Sure, they're cute—until they destroy your house. Then it's war.

"I'll bring my pellet gun. It's got a scope. That'll take care of them."

I thought about it for a minute. Could I really kill a cute little squirrel? Well, if the alternative is my house falling down around me as I sit in my recliner because they've decimated all the roof rafters and joists, yes, I guess I could. "Bring it over. Time to kill me some squirrels," I said.

Bob broke out into a huge smile. "Now you're talking." Bob is a big hunter like Rambo. I might start calling him Rambo the Second—and I'll be the Terminator.

A week later, his truck pulled in and he emerged holding a pellet gun and pellets. We walked around the side of the house to find a target so I could practice shooting it. "Damn!" he said. "A red squirrel was on your roof just now. I could have blasted him for you, but he ran into the attic."

We stood out in the thirty-degree weather, waiting for the squirrel to pop its head out, but it was too smart for us. It knew what we were up to and refused to emerge.

"Well, let's aim at something and see if you can actually hit it," Bob said.

I looked at him thinking, *Gee…he doesn't have a lot of confidence in my targeting ability, does he? I'll show him.* I grabbed the pellet gun and he showed me how to put a pellet in the chamber and where the safety was.

"Aim at the orange cone you have down there," he pointed across the yard to where I had put a cone on top of some large rocks so the guy who snowplows wouldn't run into them in the winter.

"Okay." I put the gun up to my cheek, sighted through the scope and zeroed in on the cone. I pressed the trigger and *Thwack!* I hit the cone first try. Bob seemed to be rather impressed. I was thinking a rifle would be more fun, but I didn't say it. The second time I shot at the cone, I missed. Oh, well. He told me to keep practicing and said I should open a window and shoot from inside the house when I saw one of the furry little bastards at the bird feeder.

As he walked back to his truck, I stood on the front steps and cradled the pellet gun. "All these years, they've been messing with me," I mused as I looked into the distance and thought about the sheer levels of trauma they had put me through—scampering up into the heights of the black walnut tree and lobbing the three-inch-diameter walnuts down at us as Breezy and I lay in the hammock, yelling at me in squirrel speak, or poking their furry snouts out of their hole and gloating that I couldn't do a damn thing about them living in my attic.

I lifted the pellet gun above my head, like Linda Hamilton with her badass shotgun in *Terminator*. Bob looked up at me, his hand on the truck door, probably wondering what the hell I

A red squirrel with a black walnut in his mouth, taunting me.

was doing. I let out an evil laugh, "*Heh heh heh*...Guess what, squirrels? The fun and games are over. There's a new sheriff in town." He shook his head, smiled, and drove away.

Of course, then I didn't see a red squirrel anywhere for weeks. Grey squirrels were scampering all over the place but the red squirrels were laying low. One day I went to see what Felix in his cat bed in the bay window was looking at in the backyard. *Yes!* A red squirrel was sitting as bold as day on my patio furniture, eating a black walnut. I pounded on the window and he looked up at me, completely unconcerned, calmly chewing his walnut.

"Hey, you! I'm going to *kill* you! You're lucky this window doesn't open the right direction, or you'd be toast right now."

The walnut dropped from his suddenly nerveless paws and rolled onto the ground. He stared at me, eyes wide, thinking he had heard wrong.

"No, you heard right. This is *war*. You suckers had it good in my attic, but then you had to screw it up. I've had it with you guys.

You either move out, or you're done. And I mean *done*." The squirrel looked at me in shock and horror. Yeah, he knew I meant it. Now I have to actually do it, but I'm not sure I can. The coyote was one thing; cute little squirrels are completely another.

And wouldn't you know it, whenever I write about a coyote, sure enough, one appears. As I sat here at my computer, one trotted past my window in broad daylight. I jumped up and pounded on the glass. It skidded to a halt and turned to regard me. "What do you think you're doing? Get the hell out of here!" I yelled. It continued gazing at me for a few moments, trotted a few feet, and then squatted down to pee. That was a pretty obvious message from Mrs. Coyote: *Piss on you.* The sheer in-your-faceness of it made me speechless.

Then I got mad. *Really?* I thought. *That's what you think of me? Ha! Where's that pellet gun?* I tore through the house until I found it. Grabbing it and the package of pellets, I stalked to the front door and went out into the twenty-degree weather clad in my usual jammies and fuzzy slippers. I didn't see the coyote, but that didn't mean she wasn't there. I cocked the pellet gun, slipped in a pellet, disengaged the safety, and sighted through the scope. Something was making its way through the woods on the far side of the house. I waited and waited but the damn thing never appeared.

Eventually, I got too cold and went in the house, muttering to myself. A few hours later, I spotted Rambo making his way through the backyard, wearing his camo and holding his bow, on his way to his happy place in the back forty. I opened the window and yelled out at him about what had happened and that I had tried to shoot it with the pellet gun.

"A *pellet* gun? What's that going to do?" he scoffed.

"Make me feel better, that's what it's going to do," I replied. He shook his head, turned away, and slogged off to the woods.

I have since successfully dealt with the squirrel-in-the-attic problem. And no, it didn't involve me, a pellet gun, and homicide.

I finally got smart and hired a wildlife management company, and they sent a nice young man out to remove the squirrels. He also crawled up in the attic to check for any damage but thankfully didn't find anything. Then he sealed their entry holes outside of the house to keep any other marauding red squirrels from getting any ideas about moving in.

It's not the red squirrels that are giving me headaches anymore ever since I put a stop to their fun and games when I hired the wildlife people to evict them from their cozy abode...now it's the damn grey squirrels. I have been engaged in an ongoing offensive with those furry little bastards. They have been waging guerrilla warfare with me over my bird feeders, and they seem to be winning every battle.

They eat all the birdseed and leave the feeders swinging empty in the breeze while the chickadees and other birds are left high and dry with no treats left to eat. I have tried everything to outsmart the squirrels. I bought new squirrel baffles so the squirrels couldn't drop down from the nearby branches onto the feeder. The package

Felix and a grey squirrel getting up close
and personal at the front door.

trumpeted that they were "Guaranteed to Work!" That was a huge lie. After installing the damn thing on the feeder, which took me forever since I'm not too coordinated, I had barely turned my back when the furry mafia figured out how to bypass it. Victorious, they hung onto the feeder and looked at me while they stuffed their faces. I'm pretty sure they laughed at my attempt at outsmarting them.

The next thing I decided to try was sprinkling a liberal quantity of cayenne pepper on the birdseed. I'd read birds aren't bothered by hot peppers, but squirrels can't tolerate them. Rather than douse the birdseed with the loose spice while I was still in the house, for some unknown reason, I instead waited until I was outdoors—where there was a nice, stiff breeze.

You can see where this is going, can't you? Too bad I couldn't. The cayenne pepper promptly blew into my eyes and nose, which caused me to drop the container of birdseed on the ground and race into the house to rinse out my eyes in the kitchen sink. I'm pretty sure I heard some squirrel laughter that time too. Plus, they ate all the damn birdseed, even though I had liberally coated it.

I then bought hot pepper oil and mixed it into the seeds. They ate that, too! Having not learned my lesson with the cayenne pepper, I soon realized when I put my contacts in my eyes that some of the hot oil was still on my fingers. Ouch. Back I went to the sink to rinse out my eyes once again.

Each time after finishing my newest anti-squirrel counter-insurgency tactics, I go back inside the house and sit on the arm of the couch and observe them through the window. They perch on a nearby tree branch and watch me as I watch them. After an extended stare-down, they invariably decide to go for it and try to reach the feeder. After they are foiled and fall to the ground a few times, and I laugh at them, they scamper back up on the branch, glare at me, and snarl nasty squirrel insults at me. They try again and again to reach the bird feeder until they succeed in breaching my newest anti-squirrel device, then they hang on the side of the feeder and look up at me looking out at them. And I *swear* they laugh!

Now, the squirrels have begun to climb the cedar siding on the back of the house to get to the suet feeder hanging outside the back bay window. Their sharp little claws have no problem rappelling up the side of the house. A huge raccoon did it a few times, too. That's a scary-sounding noise late at night when you're home by yourself. Thinking it was Bigfoot or maybe aliens clawing their way up the side of the house trying to get in—I think I read too much fantasy and science fiction—I snuck over to the bay window and soon came face-to-face with the raccoon through the glass. He saw me but, like all the other animals around here, didn't give a damn. I pounded on the glass to scare him away, but he ignored me and kept shoveling suet into his mouth.

My next brilliant idea was to nail thick plastic onto the siding to stop the squirrels from climbing. It looked like utter crap, but it worked fine...for a day or two. It was wonderful to see the squirrels lined up on the ground and on the tree limbs high above, completely foiled at accessing the suet feeder. They'd leap at the siding and try to get a grip on the plastic and instead slide back down to the ground. It was my turn to laugh at them. Take that, you little bastards!

Soon enough, though, the squirrels put their furry little heads together and came up with a new plan to bypass my security measures. One morning, soon after I installed the plastic sheeting, I saw a squirrel on the suet feeder, happily stuffing his face. How the hell did he get up there? I still don't know. He hung there on the feeder, swaying from side to side, calmly filling his gullet as I glared at him.

If it were only one or two squirrels raiding the bird feeders, it wouldn't be a problem. But they have now invited their extended families from the surrounding area to come and partake of the feast. I counted twelve of them the other day. Twelve!

The albino squirrel.

Next step might be the pellet gun. A shotgun, on the other hand, would certainly decimate them and would be oh-so-satisfying. Bob, who loaned me the pellet gun, told me squirrels are good eating. I may find out one of these days.

Red squirrels. Grey squirrels. I give up. I can't win. The only nice, polite squirrel I've ever seen was the albino squirrel that came to visit every so often. It was gorgeous. It never tried to climb any of the feeders. My thug squirrels soon chased it away so that they could resume their shenanigans and continue causing mayhem amongst the bird feeders.

## Chapter 31

# Donald Goes on a Trip

Several years had gone by since Donald's last emergency road trip to visit his vet. That was nice because not only was it a long-ass drive, I first had to wrestle a large, recalcitrant goat up and into the back of my SUV. When I noticed several days in a row that Donald was shivering uncontrollably, I wondered if something was wrong with him. Yes, it was December and, as December is wont to be, it was rather nippy, to say the least. Yet even after I bundled him up in an old alpaca coat, he was still shivering as he lay curled up in his nest of straw inside his garage.

I kept a close eye on him for a few days and decided it was better to be safe than sorry, so I phoned to make an appointment for him. "Can you get him here in an hour?" they asked. I thought about it—fifty miles one-way, and I still had to get the goat into my car. "Yeah, if I drive like a bat out of hell, I could do that."

Okay, I didn't say that exactly, but pretty close. I rushed outside to back up my vehicle to the front garden pond because the raised stones surrounding it were nearly as high as the back of my tailgate, and I figured I could lure Donald up onto the stones and then shove him into the back of the SUV. Of course, I rammed the bumper into the stones a few times before I positioned it close enough. I got out and opened the tailgate, so it was ready for him. Then I went to get Donald. He didn't want to get up from his snug nest, so I had to lift and push and drag him until he got sick enough of it to stand all the way up. I put his collar (a repurposed dog collar, which somehow fit him) on his neck and then grabbed onto the attached leash and tried to get him to follow me to the door. He wasn't having any part of it and looked longingly over at the straw. I was reduced to dragging him and alternatively shoving his hindquarters until I successfully got him outside. Then I had to lure him over to my car and somehow get him inside it, all the while the clock was ticking on my hour deadline. This was all far more exercise than I had anticipated having that day—actually more exercise than I anticipated having for the next month.

Once we made it over to the snow-covered garden pond, he leaped up onto the stones with no problem because the dormant rose bush was sticking up through the snow, and it looked like good eating, so he dug in. I had anticipated a problem getting him to go into my car, so I'd tossed some carrots and lettuce into the back before I went to get him. As he nibbled happily on the rose bush, I grabbed a carrot and some of the lettuce and waved it in front of him. "Look what I have here, Donald! Yummy!" He attempted to snatch it from my hands but I was far too quick for him. "Come over here and you can have some of it," I said as I tossed the lettuce into the car. I wiggled the carrot suggestively in front of his nose and slowly moved it toward the car. It was working...he was almost there...just a little farther and...*Arrggh!* He figured out that something was up and lurched back away from the open tailgate. Now I had to start all over to trick him into getting into the vehicle. Suffice it to say it took a while, but I was successful after luring him and then pushing and prodding his back end until he finally leaped up into the car, and I slammed the tailgate shut with a huge sigh of relief.

I had no idea how long this had taken, but no way was I going to make it to Zumbrota on time. Whatever. I hopped into the front seat, fired up the engine, and peeled out. I'd never had Donald loose in the back of my car—the last time I'd transported him, he'd been small enough to fit into an extra-large dog kennel. This time, he was so large that he barely fit into the back of the car. I'd worried that he would be able to get over the back seats, but he didn't have enough room. As I rocketed down the road and blasted through my small town, I hoped no one, especially the local cops, could see that I had a goat in the back of my car.

It brought back memories of when I'd had an alpaca in the back of my Jeep Wrangler years ago after picking him up from the University of Minnesota Large Animal Hospital. That time I had to drive in full rush hour traffic, and everybody could plainly see that I had an alpaca in my car. They were snapping photos and probably doing Facebook Live the whole time. I'm not sure which is worse—to be seen driving around with an alpaca or a goat in your car.

Years ago, in that same Jeep, I stuffed it full of I don't know how many cardboard flats full of chirping baby chicks. The only open spot was the driver's seat. That was when I worked in an airline cargo facility, and the managers told me that I was welcome to take them if I could find a home for them, since the shipper and consignee had both given up on the shipment. This happened in the middle of winter, and the poor little chicks had been stuck in their boxes for an entire week. The flights were so full that there was no room in the cargo bins to load them, so they were carted back and forth in the freezing weather for a week. I couldn't believe any of them were still alive, and—you know me—I was damned well going to save them if I could. After loading them up, I had to drive for forty-five minutes and the combined cheeping and chirping was deafening, not to mention the overpowering stench wafting from the boxes. Even though it was freezing outside, I rolled down my window halfway so I could breathe. I delivered them to a farmer who said he'd be happy to take them. Obviously, I'm not new to having livestock riding around with me. I have yet to stuff a mini horse into my car, although I do remember seeing photos online of someone doing that, so I'm not the only lunatic in this world, it seems.

Once I was on the highway with Donald, I saw that it was down to one lane in each direction, although no construction work was going on. Nothing like making me more stressed out than I already was. Why the hell they were doing construction in the middle of winter, I have no idea. It's bad enough in the summer. Luckily, the traffic was light, so I was able to keep at top speed while I looked out for any cops. Donald had decimated his treats in short order and was now bleating non-stop as he poked his head over the back seat and looked out at the countryside flashing by at warp speed.

Eventually, we rolled up to the vet clinic, and I went inside to let them know Donald had finally arrived. Unfortunately, it was the day they were seeing pets like dogs and cats inside the clinic, not livestock like goats. This meant Donald and I were stuck waiting out in the car, and he'd be examined outside in the ten-degree weather. Finally, the vet came out, and Donald was liberated. Good thing I'd previously placed leftover carpet on the cargo floor of the SUV and covered it with a rubber mat because he hadn't been shy about liberally dropping goat pellets everywhere. I wasn't looking forward to cleaning that particular mess up, but it would have been far worse without the carpet and mat.

It was good that this time we got Dr. Rachel because Donald really liked her, which meant he'd be less of a pain in the butt for me to deal with as I held his leash. He actually stood still as she inserted the large rectal thermometer to take his temperature, although I cringed a little. I let her know how he'd been shivering even with a heavy alpaca coat and wondered if he was sick. She completed the exam and said he could have meningeal worm, although it's rare in goats—alpacas and llamas are more susceptible. It's endemic in areas with white-tailed deer that roam my hobby farm in spades. She said it's possible he could have grazed in an area with deer droppings and picked up the parasite.

Meningeal worm is a nasty parasite that attacks the central nervous system and brain and, if not treated in time, will eventually kill the animal. There's no way to test for it other than to do a necropsy of the brain after the animal dies, so she figured it was best to treat him as if he had it. One of the few anti-parasite drugs that is able to cross the blood/brain barrier is Ivermectin, and she prescribed an oral dose for him in case that was what was going on. She said it's one of the safest drugs available, so it wasn't a problem to use it on him, even if he didn't have meningeal worm.

A horse vet had told me the same thing the day I called her in a panic after Misty had accidentally gotten dosed by the farrier with the entire amount in the syringe, which meant, instead of the 250-pound amount, she swallowed the dose for a full-size 1,250-pound horse. I was sure she was going to die, but the vet said it was lucky it was Ivermectin rather than another type of anti-parasitic because it was safe at up to ten times the recommended dosage. I had absolutely no idea about this drug prior to this, but I was really happy to hear it, and Misty had no problems, thankfully.

Donald tended to wriggle out of the alpaca coat I had been using on him since it didn't fit him correctly, so Dr. Rachel directed me next door to a store that sold livestock equipment, fencing, and calf coats. She thought that a large coat made for baby cows would fit him and keep him warmer in case his shivering was simply from being cold. I walked over to the store and soon returned holding a snazzy blue number. We attempted to put the calf coat on him, but it was far too small. We struggled to get the coat to fit while Donald did his best to foil us. If you've never wrestled a stubborn goat, you're really missing out. It's great for building strength and stamina. The vet finally managed to pull the coat over his head and onto his body. It didn't even make it halfway down his back. "I can't believe it. He's bigger than a calf!" she exclaimed. She would definitely know since she deals with cows all day long in the livestock barn. On Donald's first visit, one of the other vets had said he was the biggest goat she'd ever seen. I went to return the coat while Dr. Rachel coaxed Donald up into the back of my SUV, ready for our return trip home.

Once we arrived home, I wrestled Donald back into the garage, which was another strength- and stamina-building session, and then went online to figure out what kind of coat I could buy for a goat. I found a number of goat breeder websites, and many said they used mini horse coats for their goats, so next, I browsed horse supply websites and learned how to measure a horse for a coat. Figuring it couldn't be much different than measuring a goat, I went back out in the freezing cold to get Donald's measurements. And let me tell you, that wasn't fun. He danced around, head-butted me a number of times, and reared up, pretending he was going to stomp me. When he rears up on his back legs, he's got to be seven feet tall. It used to scare me, but he's never done anything other than rear up. He thinks he's being funny. When Donald doesn't want to do something that you want him to do—which is pretty much always—that's his playbook. And if he ever did stomp me? As soon as I managed to crawl back up from the floor, I'd make sure he'd be flat on his ass on the ground so fast he wouldn't know what hit him. It wouldn't hurt him, but it would demonstrate to him that I was the alpha goat. Who am I kidding? He will never consider me the alpha, but I can pretend. I'll never be the alpha mare, either. Misty and Sunny would never allow it. Maybe I can set my sights on something more attainable and try for alpha chicken.

As I scrolled through the websites, so many choices of colors, fabrics, and warmth factors were available that it was difficult to decide which coat to order. Eventually, I settled on a medium-weight in hunter green. That seemed to be a manly color, so I figured he'd like it. I almost went for the pink and purple polka dot one, but that would be mean. I'd deserve a stomping for that.

The weather continued to be colder than snot, and Donald's coat wasn't going to arrive for a week. I told him he'd just have to suck it up, but I did give him extra treats and lots of straw to snuggle into to keep warm. The minis, on the other hand, laugh at the cold. I swear they must have bloodlines that originated in Siberia because it could be ten below zero and a blinding blizzard, but they prefer to stand outside, covered in snow. Especially Misty.

The big day finally came. Donald's coat had arrived. Now, I had to somehow get it on him with no help. The temperature hadn't climbed above ten degrees for two weeks, and I was not looking forward to this. I suited up in my parka, grabbed the goat coat, and out I went to wrestle a nearly 200-pound goat while freezing my ass off. When I opened the door to the garage, Donald already knew something was up and do you think I could catch him? It was a complete nightmare. He ran in circles around the inside of the garage with me chasing him, and the mini horses galloping wildly because, why not?

I loudly uttered copious swear words, but I finally caught him without being run over by a speeding mini horse and quickly attached his collar. The minis were still fired up, so I decided to take him outside to try and put his coat on. I was already frozen solid. Running around like a crazy person hadn't helped warm me up in the least, but it had pissed me off quite nicely. He fought me every step of the way outside, and I had finally had enough. I dragged his sorry ass over to the corral panel and tied him to it with a short leash. He bucked and struggled the whole time, so I finally resorted

Donald looking quite stylish in his new coat.

to shoving his body against the panels using my full weight, while simultaneously trying to put the coat on him. Actually, I could have used a couple more arms. Then, I had to secure the belly straps. You'd think I was killing him or something. He absolutely freaked. "I'm trying to help you, you idiot! Don't you want to be warm? Or would you rather keep freezing your ass off? *Quit wiggling!*" I yelled.

After numerous attempts and nearly falling over backward a few times when he rammed into me, finally his coat was on, and I led him back inside the garage. His new coat fit perfectly, and he looked quite debonair. He'd never admit it, but I think he liked it. He wore it proudly all winter and didn't want me to take it off him when spring rolled around.

Ah, yes, spring. When the trees are in bud, flowers begin to bloom, and mushrooms grow like wildfire in shady, moist spots. One morning in mid-May, barely awake, I went to feed the minis and Donald. I woke up fast when I realized something was seriously wrong with Donald.

He was frenzied and circling, and his sides were heaving from his frantic panting. I watched as he ran around head-butting anything he could ram into. Misty, Sunny, the corral panels—you name it, he rammed into it. His eyes were wild, and he was acting completely crazed. I tried to get him to calm down, but I didn't think I'd be safe if I went into the pen with him.

I'd never seen him act like that, and I was scared to death. He looked like he was scared, too. I tried to figure out what was wrong with him—had he somehow been poisoned? Was he suddenly rabid? His vaccinations were up to date, so I didn't think it was rabies. That meant he must have eaten something, but I had no idea what might have caused that strong of a reaction. It was far too early in the morning for his vet clinic to be open, so I had to simply watch over him and pray. He did calm down after awhile and went to lay in his straw, so I decided to monitor him and take him to the vet later.

I checked on him periodically, and while he was no longer panic-stricken and crazed, he still didn't look right. I backed my car up to the raised garden bed and somehow lured him into the back once again, and off we drove on another road trip to the vet clinic. The day had turned out to be a scorcher, and of course, the air conditioner in my car had gone belly up, so I rolled down all the windows. Donald immediately stretched his long neck over the back seat and stuck his head out the window like a dog for the entire trip. He was obviously feeling better because he seemed to be enjoying the ride, but I wanted to get him checked by the vet anyway.

I spent the next fifty miles scrunched down in my seat, sunglasses on, praying that no one who knew me saw us cruising through town or barreling down the highway. Can you imagine if I had been pulled over by the State Patrol? I can totally see it: The trooper would mosey up to my window with his hand on his unholstered pistol, trigger finger itching. He'd give me that thousand-yard cop stare from behind his Ray Ban aviator sunglasses. His only words to me before slapping on the handcuffs would be, "Ma'am? Why do you have a goat in your car?" To which I would reply, "Ummm...Because I can?"

Donald and I eventually arrived unscathed at the veterinary clinic, and Dr. Rachel came outside to help me get him unloaded, then she examined him. Thankfully, she didn't find anything abnormal. We scratched our heads trying to figure out why he'd been acting so oddly. I mentioned that I had noticed tiny mushrooms sprouting near where he had been eating, and she thought it was possible that they were toxic. We joked about them being "magic mushrooms." One of the other veterinarians came out to say hi to Donald. He's a rock star there—everyone loves him, and he loves all the attention.

"Come on, Donald, get your butt back in the car. It's time to go home." He hopped up into the car, and I waved to Dr. Rachel as we drove away. Once we arrived home, I walked around the enclosure,

Donald with his head out the car window on arrival at the clinic, greeting Dr. Rachel with a kiss.

pulled out every mushroom I could find, and tossed them in the woods where he couldn't get at them. I probably should have worn gloves because, when I went online to find out what kind of mushrooms they were, it turned out that they actually *are* mildly hallucinogenic. The description I found online on the *ultimate-mushroom.com* website had this to say about the *Panaeolus fimicola* mushroom: "A widespread mostly inedible but not poisonous mushroom, which sometimes contains small amounts of the hallucinogen psilocybin."

Donald really *had* been dropping 'shrooms! I have a druggie for a goat. And boy, did he have a bad trip.

Sometimes I think if I tell people all the weird shit that happens around here that they'll think I'm making it up. No, I'm not. Unfortunately. The truth actually is stranger than fiction, at least in my life. What's that Chinese saying? "May you live in interesting times." Yup. That would be the story of my life.

Donald getting some love from Dr. Amy and Dr. Rachel.

## Chapter 32

# Life is Good

The sun has not yet risen on a cold and grey April morning, but light is seeping into the world. I step outside with Breezy and keep an eye out as she does her usual morning ritual. Plopping myself up onto the raised brick flower planter, I lean back against the house, holding my coffee cup. Closing my eyes, in the stillness, I hear the low bass calling of great horned owls in the distance. Geese begin honking in the nearby pond while ducks are also awakening. Cardinals are the first birds to visit the bird feeder, as they are able to see in the low light. Their trilling calls come from the birch tree above me. The flock of twenty-five wild turkeys that visited my yard the day before is now waking, grumbling and clucking, from their perches near the tops of the old oak trees across the pond. I smile at the sounds of flapping wings and lumbering flight as they ponderously launch themselves down to the ground, hitting branches the whole way. All of them gobble at once, and that's a really creepy sound to hear when it's barely light and you're sitting outside in the pre-dawn chill.

Everyone getting along: my favorite deer,
three mallard ducks, and the goose family.

Stepping outside again to do one thing or another later in the day, at one point at the bird feeders, I see several chickadees, a cardinal, and a pileated woodpecker all sharing the feeders. Shifting my gaze to the driveway where I put the corn, I notice several geese, six wood ducks, a mallard duck, three crows, and a squirrel, all together, eating in companionable silence. A deer joins them, and I marvel at witnessing so many different animals all getting along in such close proximity. This makes me think about the current political and social climate where everyone is always at each other's throats. Once again, I come to the realization that people could definitely learn from the animals.

Later in the afternoon, I see the lone goose that had napped most of the day under a big pine tree arising from his slumber and making his way to the front pond. The mallard ducks are swimming in the back garden pond. *This is so peaceful,* I think.

The day is nearing an end, and the sun is setting over the trees to the west. The wood ducks are gobbling up the last bits of corn on the driveway. Looking into the sky from inside the house, I notice three turkey vultures circling. The ducks notice them too, and, with cries of alarm, they burst into flight before I make it outside to warn them.

Standing now on the front steps, I watch the turkey vultures soar in lazy circles above me. As they swoop and turn, the waning sunlight catches the undersides of their wings and limns their feathers with flashes of molten gold and scarlet, making them look nearly phosphorescent. My breath catches in my throat; it's so beautiful. As I look upward, I tell them they are stunning. I have no idea if they understand, but I know they see me standing outside, my mouth wide open in wonder. Another spiritual moment, this time courtesy of the vultures.

The sun is now long gone, ducking below the horizon. Breezy and I are once again sitting together on the front steps at dusk. She didn't want to come inside earlier, so I joined her outside.

This is me, on the same front steps, with a dog when I was three.
Some things never change.

Night noises: ducks muttering; frogs croaking—it sounds like at least three different kinds of frogs; some kind of animal splashing through the pond shallows; geese grumbling; another animal tromping through the woods. Mosquitoes buzzing past; a few late duck stragglers flying over on their way to bedtime in the pond; fireflies flitting to and fro, bright beacons in the deepening twilight.

For years after moving here, I was too afraid to be outside at this time of night because of the coyotes, even though it has always been my favorite time. I still am afraid—that's why I'm on the front steps next to the door rather than out in the yard, so I can make a quick escape into the house. Yet I push past my fear, because this is all too good to miss.

www.ingramcontent.com/pod-product-compliance
Lightning Source LLC
Chambersburg PA
CBHW021050090426
42738CB00006B/275